# ENOUGH

*by the same author*
ROUGH IDEAS

# STEPHEN HOUGH

---

# *enough*

## *Scenes from Childhood*

faber

First published in the UK and the USA in 2023
by Faber & Faber Limited
Bloomsbury House
74–77 Great Russell Street
London WC1B 3DA

Typeset by Faber & Faber Limited
Printed and bound by CPI Group (UK) Ltd, Croydon, CR0 4YY

All photographs courtesy of the author

A CIP record for this book
is available from the British Library

ISBN 978–0–571–36289–9

MIX
Paper | Supporting
responsible forestry
FSC® C171272

Printed and bound in the UK on FSC paper in line with our continuing
commitment to ethical business practices, sustainability and the environment.
For further information see faber.co.uk/environmental-policy

2 4 6 8 10 9 7 5 3 1

'Why on earth do you want to write your memoirs? Best to keep those things to yourself. Well, so long as I'm not in it . . .'

In memory of Eileen, my mother's sister

# CONTENTS

## CHETHAM'S

# CONTENTS

## RNCM

## JUILLIARD

# CONTENTS

# PROLOGUE

Every memoir is part fiction as every novel is partly autobio-graphical. And anyway, a complete autobiography is usually boring or indecent. It's the person at the dinner table who just won't stop talking. It's the musical phrase with no breath.

Perhaps there's another way. To leave aside the grand saga of our existence and, instead, to share some vignettes, with-out trying too hard to stitch them together. There will be, there must be, gaps; and there will be erasures. Drawing an occasional veil is expected, but how to avoid writing with an airbrush, every paragraph before the make-up mirror, twee-zers to hand? Probing for the answers we don't want to hear; putting off the questions we should ask; pretending to ask them, to answer them.

One begins to write with fear – of truisms, of clichés, of lies, of mundanity. How to avoid self-consciousness when the act is to be conscious of self's history? How to transform the trembling arm-held selfie into a steady self-portrait, but yet keep the freshness of a sketch, dashed off as life dashes past? The hope is to paint a portrait that can be viewed with interest without knowing or caring too much about the sitter, as the transparent gaze or gauze of Pope Innocent X on the canvases of Velázquez or Bacon is more interesting than the pontiff's opaque life.

1

Truth and fiction. But these cannot be consciously unclear in a memoir, even if I've changed some people's names along the way for the sake of privacy. I can't write that I was born in Wisconsin in 1951 when I was born in Wirral in 1961. Scratch that. The fake always flatters. Try 1971. But a writer's words are always only symbols of reality, always a mask, ellipses . . . specks of face powder covering nothing much.

Lucian Freud's unfinished self-portraits . . . enough. But who joins him in the frame? And who do I force to join me in this mirror of my life? The sheer responsibility of writing a memoir, not to oneself but to others. Some I love are barely mentioned in these pages; others I will force before the frigid glass. How much to hide or blur? When life ends all will be hidden or blurred, but books last longer than the people they have power to hurt. And one false word can cause a war.

Laps of memory, the circle of passing years, always repeating, never the same. Traced patterns on the beach wiped smooth as waves eddy around our sometimes unsteady feet – teasers around the ankles of the rolled-up trousers. If some sand remains between the reader's toes by the end of the book it will have served its purpose.

# WIRRAL TO THELWALL

# Ridgeway

Number 45 The Ridgeway, Meols, Wirral – the first house I remember living in; I must have been no older than three. In fact, do I really remember it? Without the name having been mentioned over the years the memory would certainly be too pale. But I do recall one thing involving infant fingers that had yet not dreamt of scales. In the morning room, a room off the kitchen where the sun seemed always to stream in through a window on the side of the house, wallpaper was being removed. Mother soaping the walls, softening them, grey suds coursing down to the skirting board. Then shreds of ugly paper being torn off. They must have been redecorating. Despite my small stature I could help out, and I remember scratching at the walls and feeling a squirm of discomfort in my chest at the grating sound as the scraps of gluey paper lodged under my fingernails.

Ah, then there was the morning after one of my parents' wilder parties when those same walls were covered in shaving foam and empty bottles clinked in corners of every room. I remember no more until our next house in Birch Road and . . . well, this memory involved infant, pre-scale fingers too but it demands a different chapter, a place where the blushes can be contained.

I went to a kindergarten called Minto House, a large sandstone house on Birkenhead Road, between Meols and

Hoylake. I recall satchels and an itchy school uniform and tied tongues inside the Victorian windows where Victorian widows hammered facts tough as leather into minds supple as plasticine. Nursery rhymes tumbled out of my mouth in those years like toys out of an old suitcase, songs spat from a baby-toothed mouth. Apparently I had memorised more than seventy by the age of two. (How many are there?)

And then there were walks with my mother's sister Eileen, me pushed in the pram along the long avenue from Hoylake to West Kirby – Meols Drive, where the rich lived rich lives behind the luxuriant hedges. My luxury was 'chucky eggs', boiled firm, peeled, then rough-mashed with butter and salt and specks of dirty pepper, eaten straight out of a mug whilst still warm when we arrived back at my grandparents' house. Number 8 Derwent Road had a chilly, musty front room containing a glass cabinet filled with china (plates and cups and saucers and figurines) which rattled with every passing footstep. It was a place kept for best, reserved for visitors only. But as my grandparents never had any visitors it remained always empty. It would have been unthinkable to eat my chucky eggs in there.

## Third finger

One of my oldest, clearest memories. That longest digit, which trills so well with the thumb, the 'up yours' finger, was up his. Yes, before I was five years old I had inserted my third finger up a neighbourhood boy's rectum.

We were now living in Birch Road, half a mile from The Ridgeway, and there were games in the garden and bikes in the scrambled lanes, autumn conkers, a silver sixpence for sweets or summer ice cream cones, and I can see my bedroom. An iron bedstead, high off the ground, tall enough for two small boys to creep underneath. Make believe. It was the coal mines. Hidden from sight, sheet draped down, blind to the implications, prostate size of a pea, testicles before the Fall, we played games boy to boy. We were miners. He went off to work (or was it me? no, him). And I stayed at home, waiting for his return. And in that confusion of roles and bodies and desires and 'this is for that' and 'that is used for this' . . . then his pants were down and he turned around ('Shall I?') and I pushed my longest finger (later, I would use it to trill long at the top of the keyboard in the Liszt First Concerto during the storm in Cleveland) up his anus.

Our bodies are the miraculous homes in which we live every second of our lives. And, before taboos, we explore and look and play and gradually learn to respect. And, aged four, it seemed easier to share a body's probing than to share sweets or toys or comics. Later the finger might become a fist in the face ('fucking queer!') but not just yet. Not yet will bluebottles lay eggs on the cracks of the toffee; not yet do toys choke and break as stuffing spews out; not yet do comic books bend or tear.

'Stephen, I know what you two were doing under your bed, and it's not something nice boys do.' My mother caught us and gave me the gentlest reprimand. What is strange is that right there, in Birch Road, Meols, I knew I was gay even though I had not the slightest hint of any such concept. I felt excitement (a little) in my bones, but more, much more, I felt tenderness with another male person. And, looking back, I feel a tender gratitude for my mother's measured, sensible response to it.

## A short walk from the Beatles

Did I actually meet Julian Lennon outside the hairdressers in Hoylake in 1963? My mother told this story, that she and Cynthia were both having their hair done and I was in a pram outside, as was Julian. It was at the time when the Beatles were skyrocketing to fame, the autumn of that year: 'John has a big concert in London and I want to look my best,' said Cynthia, as the dryers blew and baked their hairstyles into place. Was this 'The Great Pop Prom' in September that year, or the London Palladium performance a month later which attracted fifteen million viewers? The couple had kept their marriage out of the press but nothing could escape the prying eyes of Wirral's perms and sets.

The Lennons were then living at 18 Trinity Road, a short walk from our own house in Birch Road. Curiously, today, about the same walking distance from where I live, lives another Beatle. Back in the 1960s Paul McCartney's dad worked with (or for) my grandfather in the cotton business in Liverpool. It's where the Beatles' early white shirts came from – strange to think of, in light of their later beards and beads. I have a signed photo from Paul from those years: an innocent scrawl across four young men in black suits and ties.

## Upstairs and downstairs

Derwent Road in Meols, where my maternal grandparents lived, a short walk from our house in Birch Road – across the railway bridge, loop around the shops and left into a quiet road of semi-detached, pebble-dash houses. Upstairs in number 8 the musty smell of old (not antique) furniture, piled-up linens in a chest and an ancient musical box. Upstairs too the counting sheep of restless nights in the back bedroom under flannelette sheets, overlooking, overhearing the railway tracks where commuter trains clattered at regular intervals beyond the high fence and the field's higher weeds. Downstairs the lamb roasting in the oven, potatoes sunbathing to a crisp in the kitchenette. Nanna's desiccated cooking. Baking too, granary bread or scones dry as a brick.

Between the two floors, at the bottom of the stairs, next to the phone, hung a tiny portrait of the queen. Probably from the year of her coronation, and about the size of a credit card before credit cards existed ('Don't buy what you can't afford'; 'If you can't pay for it, do without,' as she always said), it identified my Liverpool grandma as Orange rather than Green. A Proddy Dog. It would have been Our Lady of Lourdes in that frame at the bottom of the stairs if she'd been from the other side of the tracks but no, it was our gracious queen of Windsor, Defender of the (Protestant) Faith.

My grandparents were not at all artistic. No musical instruments of course, except the wooden musical box, but also no books and no records (or record player) either. But in their bedroom, front of the house, hung a large painting. A Constablesque scene of a rickety cottage on the sloping bank of a stream, fire glowing within, ducks paddling on the pebbled shore. When I stayed with them I would often creep into their bed in the morning, my grandfather on the right, gasping around the clock with emphysema from sixty-plus cigarettes a day, propped up on rock-hard pillows so that he was virtually upright. Easy to reach for the cough sweets at his bed side . . . next to the covered cup fizzing with dentures.

I loved this painting and I would lose myself inside its rural scene of pre-industrial-revolutionary chaos. It was large but (so we discovered after my grandmother's death and its subsequent removal from the musty frame for restoration) it was only a print. Nothing to restore. No varnish to remove. I felt part of my childhood scraped away when we found this out.

'I never saw your grandfather without his clothes on,' said his widow later. They had two daughters, my mother and Eileen, but apparently he always kept his shirt on until his pyjama bottoms were safely in place, the former's striped rudder a reliable screen of modesty. What Victorian fumbles were necessary to keep the human race from extinction! Which reminds me of the mother of a friend of mine who told me, after a couple of glasses of wine, that on her wedding night, such a good Catholic girl was she, when her husband had removed his clothes, all modesty cast aside in excited nuptial anticipation, she pointed at him and exclaimed: 'But you've only got one!' Creation's original multitasking organ confused this innocent young woman.

## Grandad and the pet shop boy

Both my father's parents died before I was born, indeed in the very year I was born. But I remember my mother's parents very well. It's actually amazing that my grandfather, George, sticks so clearly in my memory because he hardly spoke. The quietest man married to a most garrulous woman. I see his slicked-back white hair, thin on a balding crown. I see him sitting in a chair to the left of the fireplace, a grey or blue sleeveless jumper over a white or blue-striped cotton shirt, with Henry, the green parrot, perched on his shoulder. A pair of claws dug into the wool and dribbles of white shit down the knitted front. And cigarettes. Always cigarettes.

Sixty or more a day left their mark, on the ceiling and on his fingers, both stained yellow-brown, sticky as flypaper. Maybe that's why he hardly spoke. His mouth was otherwise occupied, sucking smoke from the stick of tobacco which smouldered down to a stub, then a replacement. The desperation of finishing one fag, the exaltation of lighting another; an eleventh finger pointing towards the inevitable eleventh hour. His breathing was so sharply and frequently indrawn that it was impossible for him *not* to inhale the fumes, chest heaving, shoulders rising and falling, a halo of smoke during every waking hour, every second an audible gasp . . . until his last gasp.

11

His work was in Liverpool, at the Cotton Exchange. I visited him once in his office: the leather-topped desk, the card index, the stiff-collared shirts, the waistcoats, the blotters and fountain pens, the mahogany swivel chair, the soot-stained windows . . . and the ashtrays sagging with butts and ash. As a hobby my grandfather owned a couple of pet shops on Market Street in Hoylake, a few blocks from the sea where, if you swam hard and straight and long and westwards, you might arrive at Dublin, unless the tide swept you south to Anglesey. I actually thought that one of these shops was my first home – my parents lived there for a short while, a flat above the nibbling hamsters and squawking budgies, a place of cages and musky seed. But no, I found a flyer in my father's papers:

A TRAMP SUPPER
45 THE RIDGEWAY, MEOLS
ON
SATURDAY 2ND JANUARY
1960
Oldest clothes must be worn.
These must be suitably torn and creased.

Almost two years before I was born.

## Salted sugar

If I play a trick or joke on someone I can't keep the pretence going for long. An April Fool lasts only seconds before I buckle under and give in. Whether it's compassion or cowardice I don't know. But there was the time in Derwent Road . . .

My grandmother kept her sugar in a large crystal bowl which was placed on the table during meals. I wonder why? I'm sure we only used it to sweeten tea, but there it was. And next to it was a small glass salt cellar. Their contents were indistinguishable from each other. On one occasion, just before lunch when I was alone in the dining room, I shook copious amounts of salt into that crystal bowl. Drinking tea afterwards I complained of the sugar's horrid, salty taste. It was a strange joke. 'I'll have to write to Tate & Lyle. They've always been so reliable,' said my grandmother, grimacing as she tried my tea, perplexed and distressed. I didn't admit straight away what I'd done – perhaps the jape was kept up for a couple of days – but when I did confess I wasn't especially punished beyond a stiff telling off. My grandmother was more hurt and disappointed than angry, and I believe her restraint gave me an early distaste for humour that hurts.

## Transparent machismo

One day we had all been shopping and returned home to find ourselves locked out of Derwent Road. What to do? We went to a neighbour for assistance. This man was always doing odd jobs around the street, ever a screwdriver or drill in hand. Perhaps he had a glass-cutter with which he could make an incision in the front door's frosted pane so we could reach in and turn the latch? 'Of course I can help.' A gleam in his eye, a strut in his step as he strode through the front gate and left along the path towards the front door. He was wearing a flat cap, paint-speckled tweed, and as he took his last steps up to the threshold he removed the cap, formed a fist inside it, flexed his biceps, and thrust his well-protected knuckles through the small window with an almighty punch. The glass shattered into a jagged hole and he opened the door with a flourish of triumph before going back to his house, his masculinity asserted and unchallenged.

'Heavens above! We could have done that,' my grand-mother said. 'I thought he'd have a special machine.' And as we entered the hallway, her annoyance turned to anger. There was glass absolutely everywhere. Tiny shards and splinters had showered up the stairs, along the shelves, inside shoes. It required a full spring clean to restore the house to safety.

## Vicious Henry

Henry was my grandfather's parrot. He was aggressive and ugly, with a sardonic squawk in place of a copycat phrase. He and my grandfather were utterly devoted to each other and Henry seemed miserable after my grandfather's death. The only thing that appeared to delight him was if members of the family would dance around his cage singing a catchy tune. 'Gonna dance with a dolly with a hole in her stocking' would do the trick, and Henry would begin to wheel up and down in a mild frenzy. I could never reach the point where the joy of seeing Henry jig would replace my embarrassment sufficiently for me to join in.

In later years when my grandmother came to stay with us Henry would come too. He was kept in the breakfast room near the Aga where people tended to gather. I could always escape to the piano. Except for an occasional corpse-waking screech, he simply sat on his perch and pooed onto the *Warrington Guardian* newspaper sheets lining his cage. But there was another issue. Apparently he was only truly happy when listening to Radio Merseyside, so the radio was constantly tuned to that station, at a low volume, to keep him content. Light pop music or a show such as *Hold Your Plums* would drone all day long near his perch. I could always escape to the piano.

'He doesn't like women,' said my grandmother, the rueful widow who was left to look after him. At thirty-something he was in his youthful, alpha prime: plenty of years left to peck. As she opened the cage to put a tasty morsel in his feeder dish (an apple core was a favourite) she would have to withdraw her hand in great haste before his sharp beak was able to draw blood. An apple with its pips intact was fine but a fleshy finger was the greater catch. Was it mere playfulness – like a dating couple pinching before caressing? If she'd braved the ferocity would he then have nuzzled that sharp beak affectionately against her, looking up with a beady glare barely winking with delight? She never left her hand in the cage long enough to find out and Henry glared, between the bars, the core in his claw, biting into his lunch, a malevolent

15

eye cast on the world outside his prison, the *Warrington Guardian* suddenly moist again.


## Bianowig

Uncle Tony, married to Florence, sister of my chain-smoking grandfather, was the only person in the family with an exotic surname: Bianowig. I sensed a certain suspicion around him. Wasn't he referred to as being rather 'flash' by my parents? Didn't he wear rings, and tweeds too brightly coloured and too tightly cut? He was even slightly . . . 'bronzed'. Make-up? Surely there were no tanning salons in 1960s Hoylake. He married my aunt in 1929. I think they had a childless marriage.

But he was the piano player in the family, so why did we so rarely meet up after I'd begun to learn the piano? Did my parents want to keep me from Uncle Tony? His playing as I remember was very flashy. He loved to get out musty scores from his piano bench, especially Albert Ketèlbey. Those lovely, sweet, tooth-rotting tunes: *In a . . . Persian Market, Monastery Garden, Chinese Temple Garden* – and don't forget *Bells across the Meadows*. If in doubt, add a rippling arpeggio up the keyboard (never down). Crown the roulade with a flourish of the arm, and a wink. Keep it all loose, Tony. Keep it light. Let those rings flash; let the checks on that sleeve stretch and flex. Add an extra octave in the bass; go on, you know you want to.

Did he have a gold filling or two? Was his smile a little insincere, a little . . . flash? His wife was severe and sober and heavy-set and butch. Uncle Tony had something sensitive and hysterical about him, with a kind of laughter one imagines could easily turn to tears, hilarity in company morphing into melancholy when alone.

Why didn't we visit Uncle Tony more?

## Where my caravan has (not) rested

Mother, father, aunt and uncle (Eileen and George), grandmother and grandfather, two dogs . . . oh, and Henry the parrot. All in one Sprite Musketeer caravan hitched to the back of our car, driving down the hot motorways to Cornwall. How did we all fit in? Two cars? Some on the train? Am I misremembering? The Elsan Blue porta-potty in the ramshackle awning resting on the damp grass over the earwigs. A holiday? How could anyone have thought it was something to be desired? I only remember one such trip. Did we sell the caravan after it? It nearly cost us a divorce, or three.

And the title to this chapter – one of my father's favourite songs, which I thought nothing of at the time but which now gives me a nostalgic lurch in the stomach. Our tooth tends to become less sweet as we get older (Tia Maria to claret) but some music, especially when inlaid with memories, can still give us a sudden sugar rush. George Steiner wrote that the opening bars of Edith Piaf's 'Je ne regrette rien' 'tempt every nerve in me, touch the bone with a cold burn and draw me after into God knows what infidelities to reason, each time I hear the song, and hear it, uncalled for, recurrent inside me'. The Hermann Löhr song of the caravan does something similar to me: it floods me with pain and wistfulness when I think of it. I don't even need to hear or imagine its sweet tune. The title alone suffices.

Later in life I would play this song for my father to sing – Uncle Tony had the sheet music in his piano bench along with 'Kashmiri Song' ('Pale Hands I Loved') and the Albert Ketèlbey salon pieces: exotic Middle/Far Eastern kitsch from late/post-Victorian parlours. And my father's life pre-me . . . Australia to India, Palestine and Alexandria, common stamps in a British passport for someone born in 1926. Or is there something profoundly true about the emotions of those songs in a contemporary world which can now seem smaller despite our being able to see more of it after easy flights or on facile screens?

> *Where my caravan has rested,*
> *Flowers I leave you on the grass,*
> *All the flowers of love and memory,*
> *You will find them when you pass.*

My nostalgia is not lying under the piano and hearing my mother play, as in D. H. Lawrence's poem 'Piano'; it's remembering my sitting *at* the piano, playing the sentimental songs, thinking them a little silly at the time, not asking why they meant something to my parents but knowing that it pleased them to hear them . . . then rediscovering the songs forty years later when everyone who loved them has died. These are my 'flowers of love and memory' and, like Lawrence, 'my manhood is cast / Down in the flood of remembrance, I weep like a child for the past'.

# Lollipop

For quite a while hymns and nursery rhymes were the only music in my home and head. I did have a little record player and a selection of a few bendy vinyl discs which I would play till they popped and scratched. There was also a Roberts radio – that warm-sounding, rounded-edged box in wood and leatherette out of which light tunes danced and soap operas bubbled: Frank Sinatra, Petula Clark and Cilla Black; or *The Archers*, *Waggoners' Walk* and *Mrs Dale's Diary*.

I barely remember anything about these shows, but their titles send me back in time to that post-war past: the 1960s' bright plastic optimism (plastic sliced bread, plastic frozen peas) gradually overcoming the dark era of rationing and serge, of making war then making do. The Roberts radio had pulled us through. And now, for those like me who were not there, it was a link to the past. Before the war. 'Which war?' was a constant joke of the time: in other words, how old are you? And the child falling over, scraping elbow or knee: 'Ah, poor wounded soldier.' My parents must have seen many of those maimed young men on the streets of their youth.

We'd now moved to 30 All Saints Drive in Thelwall, when I was about five. The kitchen, the sound of the radio, like the smell of the toast, floated upstairs to my bedroom. At the foot of the staircase the custard-yellow phone was screwed to the wall, rotary dial of course, which rarely rang. Except early sometimes. WARRINGTON 63708, the number so ingrained on my memory that fifty years after dialling it I can recall it like my name. My father on a business call: 'Hello, it's Colin Hough, aitch oh you gee aitch.' I still do the same. Saves time. And mistakes. I'm sure the phone was placed as far from the radiator as possible when we finally had central heating, probably to discourage us from spending too much time on expensive calls. If you stretched the flex, though, you could sit on the bottom step of the stairs and the dog could come over and nuzzle. Balancing a mug of Nescafé on the phone books.

My mother the housewife. She who hated cooking and ironing and cleaning, who preferred to be under the car in the garage, or up a ladder in a boiler suit painting the ceiling. People were (had to be) more content then, despite the ambition burning, thwarted and repressed, underneath the daily grind. The stay-at-home wife. My mother took a job as a lollipop lady outside my primary school, holding the eponymous pole aloft to allow children to cross safely. She might as well have been paid in lollipops for I'm sure the wages were lower than minimum. But she was always a gregarious woman, and actually wearing that white oilskin coat and black-peaked hat and striding out into the middle of the street carrying her metal fluorescent lollipop was theatre of sorts. She held it, propped next to a cat's eye on Thelwall New Road, with pride and a swagger – and always a cheery greeting to the crossing kids and parents. For one, traffic-stopping moment, she was all-powerful. The Ford Cortinas and Hillman Imps halted, their drivers' calves aching as they held the clutches down in first gear, ready for the continuing ride to Latchford or Lymm.

'You should have been on stage rather than me,' I often said to her, her fearlessness manifest at parties when half a hint that she might sing or play her one party piece ('Blue Moon' vamped with three crude chords) led her to open her mouth or sit at the piano with an alarming alacrity and a big smile. I really believe that every time she stepped into the middle of the road as a lollipop lady it was as if she were leaving the wings of the London Palladium, straight out centre-stage into the footlights. It's just that these were the Cheshire headlights of a Mini Cooper on a misty morning. 'Blue moon, you saw me standing alone.'

## Uncle Alf and Auntie Ethel

Number 94 Chester Road, Grappenhall. Probably in 1966. Where and when I first touched a piano. It was at the home of Uncle Alf and Auntie Ethel, a mile or so along the road from All Saints Drive. Alfred Smith was a brother of my father's mother (a farming family from Wigan) and he had a Lancashire accent as flat in vowels as the cap on his head lacked a crown. His right forefinger was flat too, deformed into a spatula by an accident at work. He didn't exactly say 'Eee, by gum' before every sentence but a visit to their house would never be complete without it leaving his lips. He was a jovial man, kind and modest and back-slappingly cheerful, unlike his wife who (don't speak ill of the dead) always seemed to me rather sour. Or stewed perhaps, like tea forgotten and steeped too long.

It was tea that brought us together, as we used to go to their house to drink it in their back sitting room. Auntie Ethel had an extraordinary pouring technique ('Just let it mash a bit longer') whereby she would dispense a drop from the pot into the cup, then heave the pot up in the air to force the leaves (never bags) to steep a bit more. Dispensing one cup might involve at least four such gestures. It worked though, if you like your tea dark and strong so you can 'stand a spoon up in it'. I was bored by these family visits but on the right wall, in that back sitting room, opposite the cream-white door, stood a brown piano with yellow keys. A little boy aged four stood eye to eye with the teeth of those keys and gently, tentatively pressed down some of the ivory tabs. My father said that I would play chords, not individual notes. Hammers hit strings, strings vibrated inside the box and the most amazing sounds entered my ears . . . and my life. I was utterly spellbound.

Nothing would satisfy me now but to have a piano of my own and to learn to play it. 'No, we're not buying a piano. You'll get bored with it and then we'll be stuck with a useless piece of furniture in the house.' I must have mentioned it constantly (I can be persistent) and in the end my parents bought me a toy piano, smaller than Auntie Ethel's tea tray. You can't tuck a proper piano under your arm, or pick it up like a tin of biscuits. This box of tinkles and jangles was definitely not what I had in mind. It was a teabag to a real piano's mountain plantation. So I destroyed it. Not as in smashed with a hammer or stamped into the ground. Dismantled is perhaps a better way to describe the process. I fiddled with a screwdriver, poked around with my fingers, pulled and prised until it . . . fell apart.

'Please, please can I learn the piano! Please can we buy a proper piano!' They got the message and one day a van turned into All Saints Drive, parked outside number 30 and delivered a German rosewood upright piano with eighty-five yellowing ivory keys and brass candlestick holders. It cost £5, and another £25 to fix up. Then my mother opened up the *Yellow Pages* to 'P' and on the same page as 'plumbers' were 'piano teachers'. Miss Felicity Riley seemed to live closest to us, one village away in Lymm, so she was phoned and booked and I began lessons.

## Orange lipstick

The Fiat 500 was born in 1949 but the modified version driven by Felicity Riley dates from 1954, when the engine moved from front to rear. A cheap, cheerful car, unlike its unmarried driver, it was the Italian rival or sibling to the British Austin Mini and the German VW Beetle.

Miss Riley drives up to our house, parks, and I stand at the window with feverish anticipation, eyes glued on the stationary vehicle with its engine now switched off. She is applying a smear of lipstick to her lips in the rear-view mirror. Orange. Bright lips that Emil Nolde would have been delighted to have been able to create from one of his more intensely vibrant tubes of paint. The powder-blue car door opens and slams and a grey tweed skirt is propelled by the spindly legs of this wiry, powdery, elderly lady up the one-and-a-half-car drive, and through the 1960s glass front doors.

I don't remember much about the lessons but I do remember the car, and especially its colour – powder blue, sky blue, baby blue. It had not the macho, Jolly Roger swagger of marine or cobalt or navy; it was not the stuff of stiff sweaters knitted against the north wind's needles; it was more the colour of a crocheted cardigan in which to bake fluffy scones or feather-dust figurines on thin glass shelves.

'A glass of water please.' My mother would oblige and Miss Riley would plop in two fizzing aspirins (stomach trouble, perhaps?). An orange kiss on the lip of the tumbler and the teacher was fully protected from any possibility of a *fortissimo* assault. After the thirty-minute lesson she was paid and left, but as I watched her from the front window walking away down the driveway to step once more into the powder-blue Fiat I would beg my mother: 'Please Mum, can I have another lesson?' I'd already memorised the pieces Miss Riley had left me for a whole week's worth of work and I wanted her to retrace her steps from the car back to the front door. Perhaps the effect of the aspirins would last through another session. But the engine was always fired up and she always sputtered off, to the top of All Saints Drive, turning left into Stockport Road. It was as if a lover was waving goodbye.

Felicity Riley (Miss), the marital status a parenthetical suggestion of restraint, a qualification of seriousness, of busyness: 'No time for all that romantic nonsense . . . It was wartime . . . My mother didn't approve . . . I was looking after my mother . . . I didn't want to *be* a mother.' The excuses of the unmarried female piano teacher, the travelling scales-woman, pupils filling her lonely days as if substitute offspring.

Although my lessons with Miss Riley were short lived and we found a better teacher – and, later, a better piano – still, it was from those fluorescent lips *à l'orange* that I first learned that Every Good Boy Deserves Favour.

## Crane's and consumption

I suppose Miss Riley came to teach me for about six months. I practised incessantly on my rosewood upright and had a small repertoire of children's pieces, but she was a local piano teacher, used to dealing with reluctant kids being pushed to learn by pushy parents. I, on the other hand, was swallowing the piano whole.

My father was in Clatterbridge Hospital, sick with tuberculosis, and on Saturdays my mother would take me to see him and then, as a treat, we'd go to the big Liverpool music shop so I could play the big pianos. The Crane brothers started their business in Hanover Street in the years just before the First World War – a five-storey building selling sheet music and instruments with a small concert hall above the shop. This performance space became the Crane Theatre in 1938 and today it is still there, renovated and renamed the Epstein Theatre, after the Beatles' manager.

One Saturday I was sitting at one of the grand, grand pianos on Crane's main showroom floor, entranced by the sounds it made, playing my party pieces, happy as could be, when a man entered the store. He stood listening at a distance and then he came over to my mother. 'Your child is very talented. Bring him upstairs to my studio.' Crane's obviously housed teaching spaces as well.

We went up in the lift and into this large room with another grand piano. I was excited but also somewhat uneasy in a way I couldn't quite understand. I was always a little afraid of strangers as a young boy and Simon Weaver seemed to me a very strange stranger. He asked me to play my pieces again and he gave me some aural tests. 'He's certainly talented but he's being taught very badly. I would like him to become my pupil.' My mother was shocked and confused. She knew I enjoyed tinkering around on the piano ('It'll come in useful at parties, you can play all the old songs' – smoke gets in your eyes as midnight approaches and another pack of Benson & Hedges is peeled open), but the idea that it was more than that had never occurred to her. 'I'll have to give this some thought, Mr Weaver, but thank you very much for listening to Stephen.'

We went back down in the lift and drove home to Thelwall. I barely remember the thirty minutes (it can't have been more) that I spent up in that teaching studio but I can still 'taste' the encounter today. There's a metallic edge and an unctuousness in my recall. It seems terribly unfair to judge someone whom I met once, for half an hour, fifty years ago, and I make no accusations (nothing happened), but I felt uncomfortable with Simon Weaver. My mother too. And she'd no idea what to do.

'Ah, I know what I'm going to do. I'm going to phone Joan Slade. She has two daughters who study the piano.' I've no idea how my mother knew Joan Slade ('I think she used to come into your grandad's pet shop') but that phone call proved to be one of the most important in my life. 'Hello Joan, it's Netta Hough here. Can I bring Stephen over to play for you? We were in Crane's the other day and Simon Weaver said that . . . and I need some advice because . . .' Some days later we found ourselves at Dovedale Road in Hoylake, a short stroll from the pet shop; and there I was in Auntie Joan's front room playing my ditties on her light brown Rogers grand piano, and there with us were her two daughters, Jennifer and Heather. Afterwards my mother told a friend of hers that the sisters fought over who would teach me and that, like Mr Weaver, they both thought I had unusual talent. It was decided (I don't know how, except Heather was always a more driven, ambitious person than her sister) that I should study with Heather.

27

## A complicated character

Whereas Miss Riley would leave promptly after my thirty-minute lesson, despite my begging my mother for her to return, I've met no one more dedicated to teaching than Heather. Where Miss Riley had guided me along a country lane on a tricycle, Heather took the controls of a jet plane. She was strict, keen, devoted and she knew her stuff. No collapsing finger joints, don't rush, that's an ugly sound, thumbs *on* the keyboard, make sure the pedal change is clean, practise slowly please, take time there, watch before that leap, rhythms, why that fingering? *A Dozen a Day*, Beringer, Czerny, metronome . . . *practise slowly please!*

The early lessons with Heather mainly took place in Hoylake in a converted garage in their garden, on a clapped-out Chappell grand piano. But as Heather was studying at the Royal Manchester College of Music (soon to change its name to the Royal Northern) she would occasionally stay over at our house in Thelwall, where I would have further lessons. I remember her practising there too. Debussy's 'Reflets dans l'eau' was a problem because our upright only had eighty-five keys and was thus missing the upper B flat required for one of the composer's more sparkling water effects. As the arpeggios rippled up and down the keyboard on page 3 – the stone's throw, the circles on the looping lake, the liquid lasso – there was an absent note. As the second arpeggio reached up to that high B flat there was a sudden hole in the texture, a thump as the fourth finger struck wood. Also she worked away at the piano part for one of the Hindemith viola son-atas. I was most disappointed when the violist eventually came to rehearse and added her line to the piano music I had grown to know and love for piano alone.

Heather Slade (-Lipkin, after marriage) was a complicated character. There are numerous tales I could tell . . . but I won't. Well, just a couple. After a recital of mine in Hong Kong years later (she had taken a job in Kowloon at the time) she came out for dinner with some friends and the concert presenter. The latter said to me at the end of the evening, 'That teacher of yours is very strange. I said to her that she must be proud to see you playing here and she replied, "Oh, I've had many more talented students than him."' Then once, when I was already in my thirties, I decided it was time to thank Heather in an emphatic way for her tremendous help and influence: 'Heather, I cannot fully express my gratitude to you. You taught me everything in those early years. I owe an enormous amount to your dedication and wisdom.' 'Well why did you leave me then? I had a lot more to teach you.'

Maybe every ambitious or brilliant person is similarly complicated, but now that Heather is, sadly, no longer alive, let's put aside her put-downs and put my gratefulness into print: I owe more to Heather than I can ever say because the person building the foundations of an edifice is all-import-ant. However famous or distinguished a college professor might be, it is at the kindergarten stage that the vital work is done because without healthy roots nothing will be solid, nothing can freely flourish.

# Hideous ferns

Visits to Dovedale Road were a treat for more than Heather's piano lessons as there would always be cakes and tea. Joan and her husband Cyril were wonderful hosts and the most demonstrative and affectionate couple, still openly caressing each other on the sofa after fifty-plus years of marriage – a contrast to my own frigid parents who couldn't sit far enough away from each other. Joan also had piano students and taught them on her thin-toned baby grand Rogers in their front room. Weirdly, it had two drawers built into the case, under the keyboard on both sides. Joan would occasionally reach into one of these drawers for a score from which to play for us – only Chaminade, it seemed. Quite extraordinary to have such a speciality. *Pierrette*, *Automne* and the *Scarf Dance*, all of which I loved and later recorded, I heard first from her fingers in Dovedale Road. She had a perky, skittish style of playing, her wrists doing cartwheels at the end of phrases, her unremoved rings sparkling in the sunlight through the net curtains. I was always so happy when we parked outside their house, especially at Christmas when I would have small glasses of sweet sherry and get giggly and tipsy, as would Joan. 'No more, Mrs Moore,' she would say with a hoot as she filled another glass to the brim from a bottle of Harveys Bristol Cream.

There was never a cross word from Joan, although Heather told us that she was ferociously strict with them, but once I made a dreadful faux pas. We'd been shopping in Hoylake, looking around for Christmas presents I think, and had gone into a gift shop that sold various trinkets and chachkas. In the corner, in a huge vase, stood some perfectly hideous bull-rushes and other ferns, artificially dyed in garish, psychedelic colours: a screaming bouquet of nausea. When we got back to Joan's for afternoon tea I gave her a big hug: 'Oh Auntie Joan, we've just been shopping and you know what, there were these horrible, brightly coloured fern things in a big vase. They were so . . .' – I turned around as I was speaking and saw in the corner, next to the fireplace, in a large glass vase – '. . . u-u-ugly'. My voice had dropped and hesitated. But it picked up again. 'Oh, not like *those* beautiful reeds.' Too late. There was only one shop in Hoylake from which she could have bought her reeds; and there was only one shop in Hoylake in which I could have seen *my* reeds.

## Mompou: The young boy not in the garden

We had few records in the house before I started my piano lessons, indeed I only remember children's ditties, Kenneth McKellar singing Scottish songs, and the soundtrack for the newly released movie *The Sound of Music* . . . The hills (UP) are alive (HELD) with the sound of mu- (STRANGE HARMONY)-sic. I was able to tell Julie Andrews decades later that her voice was possibly the first recorded music I heard. Oh, and, astonishingly, we had a two-LP set of *Irma La Douce*, the musical not the film. My mother often mentioned with delight that she'd been to see that show before I was born. I think it might have been the only time she'd seen a musical in the theatre and those records were a souvenir of the evening out. I was always sad when she mentioned *Irma La Douce*. It seemed to symbolise a life unfulfilled.

But as soon as I started to learn the piano with Miss Riley, or perhaps when I switched to Heather Slade, my parents started to buy classical records from Dawson's in Warrington. *Clive Lythgoe Plays* was the very first, a mixed recital on the budget Music for Pleasure label. Copyright 1968, so we must have bought it hot off the press. I remember its green background with a photo of the pianist wearing a ring and a woman's watch. Also wearing a tie, which dates it, because by the time of his 1976 Edward MacDowell recording Clive had a shirt open a button or two more than strictly necessary, revealing a Native American choker and a bed of chest hair. In both he had a tan (I imagine without a tidemark) and nut-brown hair not dissimilar to mine. I used to look at his hands and hold mine against the photograph and wonder when my fingers would grow to that size. I wasn't too keen on the watch though.

It was a varied programme, the first piece being the *Fantaisie-Impromptu* of Chopin, then other light delights. Rather unusually there were two pieces by the Catalan Federico Mompou on this album and I was entranced with their lyrical charm, especially 'Jeunes filles au jardin', from the composer's 1918 *Scènes d'enfants*. I learned this little piece at the time and have played it more than any other over the years. It's the perfect encore, the perfect after-dinner truffle, the perfect piece to play at that party when I've had a few too many drinks and am incapable of playing anything else.

I was inspired by that record to work at the piano ever more, to the point when my mother had to drag me away: 'Stephen! Go out into the garden and get some fresh air,' she would cry. On a trip to Chester Zoo, supposedly a treat, I walked about looking distractedly at the lions and tigers, my fingers drumming on my chest. I just wanted to get back home, inside my own cage, with my piano.

## The most important record I owned

As my parents bought more LPs, they also bought a teak box on spindly legs. The radiogram: an all-in-one unit designed to complement a sofa or coffee table, containing a turntable, two speakers and space to store a decent number of albums. My excitement was tremendous every time I opened the hinge, careful that it didn't fall and trap my fingers. The LPs quickly stacked up inside, then spilled outside in piles underneath and against the wall as my father bought more and more. We were two sponges. Solomon playing Beethoven's First Concerto, Moura Lympany in the Grieg and Schumann concertos, and a mixed album called *Toccata*, a thrilling collection of fast pieces played by Werner Haas.

But the most influential record I've ever owned was *Keyboard Giants of the Past* from RCA with notes on the back by Abram Chasins. An angel must have been in Dawson's that day, hovering around the classical section, guiding my father's choices. This record became a constant companion, and as I listened repeatedly to every track my pianistic taste was shaped, in those earliest, most formative years. Although they were already dead (all of the selections were from 78s recorded before the Second World War), these pianists became my mentors, and their musical inflections became part of my own expressive dialect. I often warn students about the dangers of listening to too many recordings, and this is true if it means taking particular interpretations and trying to copy them. But this record opened a door to a different period, a time closer to the composers' own, and enabled me to absorb a style of playing which (like all music) is impossible to notate and which is in peril of disappearing. Moreover, such was the individuality of the players from that era that there would not be one thing to copy anyway, even if you were to try.

Gabrilowitsch was the first track, playing Bach/Saint-Saëns' 'Bourrée' in B minor (strangely mislabelled 'Gavotte'). His playing had a wonderful spring in its step with a transparency of texture in every shining note. Other tracks of his were Percy Grainger's *Shepherd's Hey* and Delibes' *Passepied*, but more than all of them I loved his own *Caprice-Burlesque*. This was my introduction to a kind of romantic genre piece which I found utterly absorbing for many years – I recorded this very example early in my career on my first *Piano Album*.

Then came the Lhévinnes, Mr and Mrs, in Mozart's Sonata for Two Pianos K448. I would later study with the assistants of both husband and wife at Juilliard. And my first experiences of Wagner were later tracks, Olga Samaroff playing *The Ride of the Valkyries* in Ernest Hutcheson's arrangement, and Paderewski playing Liszt's arrangement of the Spinning Chorus from *The Flying Dutchman*. The Polish pianist was also represented on the album by Debussy's 'Reflets dans l'eau', then more French water from the one who was to become my favourite pianist, Alfred Cortot, playing Ravel's *Jeux d'eau*. Captivating sparkle and finesse, although it was not the Cortot I came to love later in the more neurotic worlds of Schumann and Chopin. Does he miss Ravel's final bass note? I always now hear this piece ending in B major because of the unclear final chord on the hissing 78 transfer. De Pachmann playing Mendelssohn's *Spinning Song* – silk-spun needlepoint in a world of knitters. And, to end the LP, one of the greatest tracks ever preserved on disc, Rachmaninov playing his own transcription of Kreisler's *Liebesleid*. Chasins, in his note, recalls playing this piece for Rachmaninov and admitting to him that he found it deceptively difficult. 'Difficult? It's impossible!'

Along with this LP I devoured Harold C. Schonberg's book *The Great Pianists*, a roadmap for a country where I was already at home. I wrote in my neatest handwriting in the flyleaf: 'This book never fails to inspire and instruct', a pretentious aside from a ten-year-old. I ripped out that sheet in my more knowing, self-conscious, self-righteous twenties. And now, having passed sixty (and perhaps more tolerant and carefree), I rewrite it here. Our moods have seasons and fashions . . . along with our tastes.

## Heterosexual nocturne

Very soon after starting my studies with Heather I was entered into some local competitions, or festivals as they were called. I remember Liverpool and Crosby, and Bromborough Festival, my first, where I won first prize (a silver trophy) playing *A Knight on Horseback* by Eric Thiman. The soprano Susan Bullock playfully reminds me when I see her that she took part unsuccessfully in one of those festivals along with me. Her failure in the under-elevens piano was eventually to be Wagner's gain, of course, and she would, as Brünnhilde, ride a mightier horse than Eric Thiman ever dreamt of.

There was another teacher doing the rounds with her students at these competitions – I think her name was Gloria Tumelty. I never met her but she couldn't even be mentioned in the presence of Heather. It was my first experience of the bitter jealousy that often arises in the piano teaching world: 'She has no idea about technique. Her students are badly taught. They bang,' and so on – totally irrational and unfair assessments of a colleague. I looked at Gloria from afar with fear.

Anne Yardumian and Dina Bennett were the two students I remember, and both played the Chopin posthumous E minor Nocturne . . . very beautifully, I thought. I was a little in love with Dina, whose black curly hair and shy smile are still associated with that doleful piece for me. I wanted to play it too, but somehow it was so associated with Gloria's studio that the piece itself was tainted for Heather.

I watched Dina's supple hand shape the left-hand arpeggios with a strange longing.

## Could this be the new Mozart?

Beyond those local competitions Heather had greater ambitions for me, and I was entered after only a year studying with her into the National Junior Piano Playing Competition. I lived and breathed only for and next to the piano and I must have made pretty fast progress because I won the North-West round and was invited to take part in the finals, which took place at the Purcell Room at the Southbank Centre on 16 December 1969. As this venue only opened its doors in 1967 the paint must barely have been dry when this young boy with wide eyes and short trousers arrived to play. It was my first visit to London and my grandmother, who had trained as a tailor, made me a new suit for the occasion – dark brown lightweight wool in a snazzy, lapel-less design. I don't think we stayed overnight – I have no recollection of a hotel. I do remember arriving at Euston Station, itself only reopened in its refurbished form a year earlier, and then somehow I was on stage playing on a wonderful concert grand Steinway, which was probably my first. But my clearest memory is the post-competition press conference when a bossy Fleet Street photographer, fag hanging from a cynical lip, forced me to sit on a pile of phone books on the piano bench for the shot, reducing me to tears as I wobbled on the unstable platform. I was comforted by

Heather, who was wearing an Audrey Hepburn-type outfit complete with broad-brimmed hat. What a strange group we must have looked! At least my grandmother didn't bring Henry the parrot along too. 'Could this be the new Mozart?' enquired the *Daily Mail* the next day, where I appeared in its pages with a tear-stained face in my cute brown suit.

I played Bach's three-part Invention in B Minor, two Chopin mazurkas (op. 7 no. 1 and op. 68 no. 3) and Prokofiev's 'Attrape qui peut' from his *Musiques d'enfants*. I have a tiny six-inch LP from this competition, given to each competitor, with both my performance and Gerald Moore's comments. He was the chairman of the jury, which also included Louis Kentner and Joseph Cooper, and two things are of note: Gerald Moore says that, although the youngest competitor (me) has not won a prize, 'we want to highly commend him. We are delighted with his playing and we think he has great potential.' The other thing which literally sticks out is the last note I played. This little Prokofiev children's piece ends with a unison F in both hands, but with *crossed* hands, a trap waiting to snag youthful fingers. With a certain flourish I concluded my performance . . . but on an E and an F, a harsh, strident discord. I still recall a gasp from the audience and my horrified face as this jarring interval filled the hall.

## Pink stilettos in Criccieth

Until that first visit to Euston I don't think I'd travelled more than fifty miles from where I was born – if that. But I do recall holidays on the coast of Wales (or was it just one, in Criccieth?) and I remember Judy nipping my buttocks as I played on the edge of the sea. Judy, our Border collie, had small but sharp teeth and sheepdog instincts.

It was in Criccieth, aged about six, that I had one of only two cross-dressing experiences in my life. My homosexuality has never found expression (or refuge) in wanting to dress up as a woman. Camp is many (wonderful) things, but it usually has at its root a desire to shock and to cause outrage. Camp takes delight in poking a stick inside the cage of normal life, at disturbing the yawningly conventional, of making fun of the serious, or, more accurately, the dreary.

Pink stilettos (you see, placing those two words at the start of a new paragraph is already a gesture of camp). I was bought a pair, at my insistence, when we were on holiday in Criccieth one summer. I took the shoes eagerly out of the box, strapped them on, and proceeded to walk into every ice cream parlour along the promenade in those wonderful shoes, alerting onlookers with an air-prodding forefinger (in case they'd accidentally missed the sight) to look down at my feet. Their gasps of amusement or horror caused as much delight to me then as recalling the occasion does to me now. Oh, and they weren't just pink: they sparkled with glitter as well!

There was also the occasion, around the same time, when I won second prize in the fancy dress contest at Thelwall's Rose Queen Festival. This time I was Liberace holding a candelabra in my infant hands, dressed in another suit made by my grandmother (black velvet dotted all over with sequins and studs and brocade – it appears on the cover of this book), escorted along the street by my mother dressed as a man with a moustache. I have the photo still and I do look a little awkward, looking at/away from the camera, whereas my mother simply *exudes* confidence in her male costume. Indeed, her wardrobe was increasingly emptied of skirts or dresses as the years passed.

## All Saints Drive

Number 30 All Saints Drive, Thelwall, was my home from age five to sixteen. It is at the crest of a hill so if you let go of the brakes on your bike (with maybe a couple of revolutions of the pedals) you will course down past Moore Avenue, and you may make it all the way to All Saints Church if your wheels are well oiled and your balance is good. As you grind to a halt before Thelwall New Road's intersection you will have passed the houses of the Sheppards and the Monks and the back entrance of Thelwall County Primary School. In the other direction from our house, upwardly inclined, is Stockport Road. Keep going beyond it up a small hill, then over the Bridgewater Canal, then through open fields, and you'll be in Weaste Lane. We would do that bracing walk on many a wintery day: crisp leaves under muddy boots, dogs straining on leashes, farm smells, rosy cheeks.

There was a large tree outside our house which seemed immense to me when we moved in. At its base were tipped grass cuttings which formed a mound of compost up the trunk. From the tree to the front door there was room for two cars to park, and on the grass next to the tree there was room for a couple more when we had visitors. Through the front door (garage to the right) ahead to the kitchen, left to the dining room and back to the front to the sitting room, joined by glass concertina doors (hideous, later removed). Up the stairs (phone at bottom) directly to the toilet, left the bathroom, left and back my bedroom, left again my parents' bedroom, left and round the little box room, always cold, usually empty.

I became me in my bedroom at All Saints Drive. Doubled in height, voice broke, didn't do the homework I should have, listened to my pop records, and for a while . . . I looked. Gazed out at the night sky before getting into bed to sleep, or rather gazed at what lay under the night sky, behind the windows of the neighbourhood boys. From my nighttime bedroom I could see the frosted glass. Double-frosted after steam of bath or shower. Lights off in my room and my curtain a slice open. Gazing. On my knees. And I see flesh shaped like a man's body. I see the outline through the obscure glass. He's flexing in front of the mirror, then a punching. Shadow boxing. Vicious jabs into the air. It would be into my face if he knew I was watching him. The television is on downstairs, a roar of laughter from a sitcom, a blare of trumpets and hi-hat cymbals. Parents safely out of sight. Light goes off in his bathroom. Light goes off in my stomach. But then, before I get off my knees at the cramped window, it lights up again. Torso behind the frosted frame again. A towel streaming through the air. All so blurred. All so beautiful.

# The long garden

Our back garden at All Saints Drive seemed enormous to me when we first moved there. And something of its summer shadows is more memorable to me now than the house from which they stretched. Out the back door and there was the coal bunker next to a fecund patch of mint. When we had roast lamb for Sunday lunch some of this aromatic bush would be plucked, mashed and sweetened, one of the few edible things we grew in a garden that could have stocked a greengrocer's.

We could play badminton on this lawn. The dogs could race around, and leave steaming piles of poo, lethal mines in the uncut grass. We erected a tent there. Did anyone sleep in it? There was hoeing and planting, and I remember lupins. Why does my heart surge with sadness when I think of them? The shape, the bells of bloom, the wonder that they stood whilst my family wilted. There were also vast tufts of some vivid orange flower which grew like a weed. There was an apple tree and a pear tree but I don't think we ate the stunted, flavourless fruit. An incinerator where autumn rubbish could be burned was at the bottom of the garden. I remember tossing three volumes of Henry Miller into the flames once, when my Puritan fervour was burning brightly:

*Sexus*, *Plexus* and *Nexus*, ordered from a local bookshop. I never read them but knew they were meant to be wicked. I'm sure their author would have been most amused at this adolescent's raging bonfire.

The carpet and the curtains of our house remain clear in my memory. Busy as bees and similar colours, brown and orange and beige and honey-gold, buzzing in dizzy, swirling patterns. The wallpaper was busy too, paler colours of course, but still spiralling around the rooms, the clashing patterns complementing the arguments between my parents.

The two downstairs rooms were open-plan, not unusual in a house built in the swinging sixties, and there were two glass sliding walls/doors/windows which would meet crankily with a bump in the centre after a rocky ride on a rough rail. Their smoked glass panes gave privacy to all but shape and colour, although there was no limiting the sounds from my piano. We switched the position of the instrument around from time to time, beginning in the back dining room with the first upright and ending up with my Yamaha C3 in the front room. I can see Mr Jones, the elderly piano tuner, with his rusting tools, and I can smell his worn, grey woollen trousers, caked with urine. He had a bald head which seemed to be covered with brownish-yellowish leather, not skin. He lived alone. Not the marrying type? His arthritic fingers were like gnarled hammers as they knocked each note into tune. He always played the same piece when he'd finished his work: Mendelssohn's C minor *Song without Words* (op. 38 no. 2). Strange choice when I think of it.

Our fireplace had a miniature statue on the hearth of Michelangelo's David, in polished, dark-grey mottled stone. Maybe marble. Shining buttocks next to the coal scuttle. Real coal for years was dragged in from the bunker by the mint bush. Those frigid mornings with clinkers and dust and pre-washed faces and haystack hair and cold cold before the Nescafé granules dissolved with a steaming sizzle into the chunky mugs and the toast burned under the grill and the (thick-cut) marmalade jar was prised open, resisting the stick of the rim's sugar-orange, then delving inside for a knot of peel to knobble over the melting butter.

When did we get central heating so that the bedroom windows on winter mornings would not have a crust of ice on them?

## Choccie

In that garden of All Saints Drive lived Choccie, our guinea pig, a chocolate-brown creature of perpetual nervousness and vulnerability. He seemed always to want to escape, from his cage, from the pen we had built for him so he could nibble on fresh grass, from life itself. I think his coat was one of the most beautiful things I've ever seen, a deep, rich colour, thick through to the skin in prongs of a thousand mottled shades. He didn't like being picked up – holding him was like balancing a quivering jelly on a small plate. There was a kindness in his eyes and a plea for kindness from me (don't hurt me, don't drop me, don't squeeze me), but also a kind of gratitude when he could relax into the palm of my hand, sensing safety, intuiting that patience on the hand would mean quickly restored independence in the bush.

Then one day he escaped. I could imagine his terrified sprinting, through the flower borders, through the wire fence, through the neighbouring gardens. An escape from what? From the feast of fresh grass we laid on for him? From the cosy nest full of Sunday newspapers and fluffy cotton wool? From the crisp carrots and freshly replenished water? Sometimes escaping is not knowing where you want to arrive at, more than knowing why you want to leave. Choccie would have trembled in confusion until the last flinch, into the mouth of a predator or under the wheel of a passing car. I can still recall the musky smell of the straw and the twitching of his whiskery nose. And the spelling of his name.

## Coffee and being powsh

I always loved it when my mother said, 'So-and-so is coming round for coffee this evening.' I knew that I'd be able to sit there and listen to them gossip. Nothing malicious, but just that wonderful, soothing round of, 'Oh my heavens, did she really say that?' 'I can't believe it. Mind you, it was always on the cards.' 'I knew it wouldn't last long.' 'You can't trust a thing she says.' Coffee and biscuits, usually McVitie's digestives or ginger nuts. I liked the latter because you could dunk them in the mug of coffee for quite a few seconds and they would still hold together, soggy on the outside but still chewy in the middle.

Coffee in our household was Nescafé granules over which was poured boiled milk from a saucepan. Watching. The crescendo of panic as the milk bubble-bubbled on the sides before rising up the wall of the non-stick pan. Usually we turned off the gas or lifted up the pan *just* before the potential disaster of the creamy lava spilling into the elements of the stove. For the best flavour the pan should be removed just before boiling point, to allow the heat to subside, to let it calm down to quietened froth. Then poured gently on top of the granules with a hiss. We never had the powdered kind (Mellow Birds) – it was considered too lower class. No, regular Nescafé was our usual brand, but then (perhaps my father had got a rise) we changed to the slightly more expensive 'Gold Blend'. The other Nescafé option, 'Blend 37 Continental Roast', was considered a little risqué for a house in All Saints Drive, Thelwall. Too much of the unbuttoned shirt and the garlic bulbs strung around the shoulders about it, too *foreign* somehow. Even if coffee beans did not exactly grow in our back garden, we still needed to feel comfortable with their domestic provenance from the shelf at the Co-op. At one point my grandmother discovered coffee bags – real ground coffee. I was rather astonished at the development of her taste until I saw her dunk one in the hot water for three seconds (already too long) and then fill half the cup with milk. 'You can use them a number of times,' she said, each time weaker and more insipid. The post-war rationing era cast a long shadow on that generation.

'Oooh how powsh' (rhymes with gauche) was the exclamation with a range of items: avocado pear, as we called it; then lasagne in the early days, pasta no longer from a tin on toast but actually a real main course. Heinz spaghetti for lunch. I used to add grated Cheshire cheese as it simmered on the stove so it became light pink and creamy, and sometimes stringy if it stayed on the flame too long. I can't remember the first time I had real pasta but I'm pretty certain it was lasagne – probably a frozen food packet, but still a little more exotic than Findus fish fingers or the peas and oven chips we might have bought from that same freezer in the supermarket.

I only remember alcohol coming out of the cupboard at Christmas: Tia Maria, Drambuie or Benedictine, in miniature bottles. We never drank wine. The two large bottles in the cupboard were Johnnie Walker Red Label (good for colds when mixed with sugar and hot water), and Harveys Bristol Cream. I think our bottle of the latter lasted us for years. Again, with sherry, like coffee, Emva Cream was too common, whereas a fine fino was too powsh. I pretended to like Tio Pepe when it was on offer at friends' houses over Christmas, thinking it would make me seem sophisticated. I still hate it today; knives in the mouth.

## Fatty foods

Food in our house was dreadful. Everything was frozen, fried or boiled to a paste. Sprouts in particular were left to liquify as they bobbed up and down in the bubbling green water as if trying to avoid drowning. Then drained into slime, they looked like comatose slugs as they were spooned onto the plate. Let's have a fruit salad. Opening the cans of mandarin oranges and pineapple chunks and peach slices and half-pears, spearing them with a fork and, dripping syrup onto the tablecloth, pouring a glug of evaporated milk like a moat around the fake fruit. Sometimes ice cream instead, a yellow brick of Wall's, setting teeth on edge around our colour-stained, frost-swollen tongues.

I grew up between the flavoursome years. Before the Second World War people baked their own bread, and in the twenty-first century people buy nutty, seedy loaves from artisan bakers, but in the 1960s and 70s . . . why bother with a bread knife when the loaf is ready from plastic bag to toaster in one pinch? The chip pan was permanently on alert on the side of the stove, ready for action, its lard coagulating. As Stuart Hall began the round-up of local news on *Look North* it would be slid onto the flame before a lowering of the netted basket of sliced potato into the smoking, bubbling cauldron.

There was a danger to this, though. I remember being warned of the overheating chip pan, the overturning chip pan ('Take a damp tea towel and throw it on top if it catches fire'). But I knew even then, by instinct, that there were other dangers too, transmitted deep inside the body: the clogged arteries, the failing heart, acne's eruption, stomach's expansion. Yet when the glistening chips were shaken onto our plates, moistened with a sprinkle of Sarson's malt vinegar, all seemed good again. The evening of television could continue, the avoidance of homework, the stoking of the fire, the sinking into the sagging sofa.

Tea was always good though, real leaves, two-thirds Assam and one-third Earl Grey, a strong pot, steaming bronze in the almost-pint mugs. Masonic souvenirs, with my father's name on them in gold letters from when he was a Grand Master of Hilbre Lodge. But one night the grease factor was taken to the ultimate level. My father, diagnosed with gallstones, was given the choice of an operation or drinking a pint of olive oil. I was asleep and so not around to witness the torture he went through that night as he sipped relentlessly on the bottle, nausea retching his stomach, wave after wave of rising vomit, eyes watering as his lips met the bottle once more. I never asked him about the process but he proudly showed me the gallstone later. No knife had been near his body but he'd spent a few hours at the gates of hell.

## Eating on Sundays and Jean Sheppard

I loved Sunday lunches in my youth. It was the one meal of the week that was properly cooked and it was always roast meat – alternating beef, lamb, pork and chicken. Colman's English mustard with the beef, mint sauce with the lamb, Bramley apple sauce with the pork, Ocean Spray cranberry sauce with the chicken. And after lunch, the Sunday papers – *Observer* for Dad, *Sunday Times* for Mum (not only on matters of religion did they fail to agree) – and often a tabloid as well, with scurrilous front-page stories about sex and film stars.

But the Sunday lunches I really loved were when we were invited out to someone's house. Jean Sheppard taught at my junior school, Thelwall County Primary, and she lived a two-minute walk away from us, down the hill of All Saints Drive. It was only after I went to Chetham's at the age of ten that we socialised freely, and we used to go to her house for meals at least half a dozen times a year. Jean was a central part of my childhood, from the lessons I had with her in class, to hymn practice, to school assembly when I played the piano, to the church choir where I both sang and played the organ on occasion. I found a lot of my time at school traumatic for one reason or another but Jean was always a kind face – a great teacher, firm and disciplined but also warm and good-humoured. Much later in life she became a lay reader in the Church of England and right up to her premature death she would visit my mother once a week in the nursing home. My mother requested in her will that Jean be the joint officiant at her funeral, but Jean died first, suddenly, before my older mother. To walk down the path of the Sheppards' house in the 1970s was always a joy for me, and if I pass the house today I can still smell the potatoes roasting.

Jean's husband, Edward, was a gentle, gracious man with a kind smile always on his lips and comfy slippers always (it seemed) on his feet. He was large-framed and would appear in the doorway after the bell had rung, wearing a grey pullover pulled over a substantial stomach and a neatly knotted tie. He would invite us inside and, after sitting down with a sherry, would tell many amusing anecdotes about Sir Thomas Beecham or Sir Malcolm Sargent (strange how so many people from his generation who loved music fell under the spell of Sir Malcolm). Their son, Andrew, was about the same age as me, and when we tired of the adults' conversation, we'd play board games or spin records or, at Christmas time, build snowmen in the garden.

Back at home we didn't have a proper evening meal on a Sunday – I suppose we were still meant to be full from the roast and two veg earlier. So we had hot buttered crumpets or teacakes or various other kinds of cakes by the fire. It sounds nice and cosy from the distance of many decades but the darkening twilight and the smell of toasting makes me sick with melancholy to this day. It's the horror of school the next day, a feeble attempt to catch up on homework, the early rising in an unheated house, and the car journey to the bus journey from Flixton to Long Millgate. I'm not sure that that Sunday late-afternoon sinking feeling will ever leave me.

## Chubby Cheeks

No one was a greater friend to me between the ages of about eight and fifteen than Winnie Monk. She was also a teacher at Thelwall County Primary School, but only just: on the verge of retirement and brought in to supply. I don't think I had more than one class with her. But she had a piano at home, and she knew I played the piano, and she had no

children. I would go to her house (on the same street as both
Jean Sheppard and me, All Saints Drive) and we'd play duets,
talk, do some embroidery and watch telly. She would make
me cheese on toast (her own recipe, grated Cheshire mixed
with milk and tomato ketchup and ground into a paste) and
we became great pals.

The Star Folios. Winnie had a number of these Victorian volumes, two hundred pages or so of piano pieces from
a Chopin waltz or a Schubert impromptu to transcriptions
of a Suppé overture to more saccharine sweetmeats like *The
Maiden's Prayer* or *Elves at Play*. When every home that had
a sideboard had a piano, collections like these sold in huge
numbers. Winnie made me sight-read everything ('Go on
lad, you can do it'; 'Don't miss out the twiddly bits') and soon
I became fluent. Billy Mayerl was one of her passions and she
encouraged me to swing (or rather ge-dung) the characteristic left-hand accompaniments to his starched white collar,
white man's jazz tunes. *Marigold, Bats in the Belfry, Autumn
Crocus* . . . so many. We'd take the bus into Warrington and
spend hours in Dawson's music shop looking at sheet music
or records and then have an ice cream soda at Broadbent's on
the next street.

'I used to vote Labour but as you get older you have more
sense.' The *Daily Express* and, later, the *Daily Mail* were
always well thumbed in her home and she was forthright
in her opinions. Her husband, Roger, always scared me a
bit. He was jovial but slightly fierce – he'd been in the army
and it showed. A defiant moustache and a pipe clenched

tightly between his teeth. He knew Winnie and this boy shared something in which he could have no part. She was a strong woman but he was stronger; he didn't like music and he hated her playing the piano. He watched exactly the TV programmes he wanted and, after retiring from work, he moved the two of them to Norfolk where he could cruise the Broads on his narrowboat. She was absolutely loyal to him but she did once admit that she didn't want to move away from Thelwall. She was forced to sell the piano too – 'Now that I'm home all day I don't want that racket in the house,' said Roger. After she moved we always spoke around Christmas time, but I rarely saw them again.

'Now I've got something to say to you, Stephen. Pay attention! You need to be careful about older boys. They might ask you to . . . er, do things with them. I'm not going to say more, but it's something *disgusting*, and you must say no.' I sort of knew what 'things' she was referring to, although no boys had ever made such a suggestion to me. I always wondered where this warning had come from – was it from Roger's army days, a rejected grope in the forests of Burma?

Chubby Cheeks, I called her. I loved her dearly, but I was scared of (embarrassed by) the sadness underneath the romp of our Billy Mayerl swing tunes, or the sizzle of the cheese toasties. I never saw her cry but as I watched her sitting in an old leather chair gazing out the rear window through the grass to the far fields beyond I wondered if she was turning away to hide her tears.

## Empress

I've spoken of Jean Sheppard and Winnie Monk, both important teachers for me, but more so outside the classroom, after I'd moved on, than in the school. Then there were the headteachers at Thelwall County Primary, figureheads of authority whom children only dealt with at a distance . . . unless they got into trouble. The headmistress who was in charge (words not lightly chosen) when I first became a pupil there was Miss Constance Bradburn. Her name came instantly to mind but I couldn't remember her face until a friend sent me a photo of a line-up of teachers from my years there. I recognised and could name nearly all of them, and there, in the midst, Miss Bradburn sat like Queen Victoria amongst her subjects, as imperious as that monarch, and with no sense that she was merely in charge of a small school in a small village in a small county. 'Empress of India? Give me China too.' She only had to walk into a room and there was an instant hush (even the teachers seemed scared of her), but I don't remember any physical violence or even a raised voice. She just had that magnetism which commanded: 70 per cent respect, 30 per cent terror. Like Miss Riley she was an unmarried woman whose life and energy found meaning only in her pupils. She died quite soon after she retired: a life outside school was a life not worth living.

Then after her was a total contrast: Mr Leslie Jones. He was the first 'camp' man I knew. He would look at you, pause, then toss his head away with a pucker of the lips and a slight movement in the hips as he walked off – a preciousness, a sense of the outrageous, a humour ready to sting, an X-rated sensibility. I loved him. He seemed always to be smoking (Embassy blue label, as I remember) and he wore a large signet ring on one of his yellowed, nicotine-stained fingers. Pale blue suits come to mind, with that tendency they have to fray and snag and stain which suggested polyester. A broadly knotted tie, and I'm sure he had buckles on his shoes. I could tell he could be quite nasty and he was never actually warm to me. Pity, because I so wanted him to like me. I remember once saying to someone within his earshot that a certain fish tank was 'murky'. 'Oooh, it's murky is it?' Lips pursed and hips shifted to the left, limp and louche. 'Well who's going to clean it then?' And he flounced off down the hallway. Nevertheless, even if he'd expelled me from school, just one drag on the flaming fag, ash flicked with a tapping forefinger, lips pursed, dust then disdainfully brushed off his powder-blue trouser leg . . . well, I would instantly have forgiven him.

It was with no surprise whatsoever that I later learned he'd abandoned teaching schoolchildren and was working as a comedian on an ocean liner. He'd served a useful apprenticeship as headmaster of Thelwall County Primary School.

# Colours of springtime

## Colours of Springtime

*Green for the leaves that grow on trees,*
*Blue for the clear blue sky,*
*Yellow are the sunshine rays,*
*White for the clouds floating by,*
*Grey for the rabbit that lives in a burrow,*
*Brown for her big round eyes,*
*Red for the fox that waits on prey*
*On my beautiful springtime day.*

This was my first published poem, in *Runcorn and District Schools – A selection of young people's writing – Summer 1970.* I was eight years old. I can recognise myself in this poem: a little sentimental, a little quirky, not just in the fox about to do something nasty in the final 'colour' of an otherwise idyllic day, but also in the change of rhyme structure and the poem's hasty ending – a lucky escape from the lurking fox, perhaps. And why a female rabbit?

Creative writing was always my favourite subject at school. I loved the way I could express my inner life fearlessly: the smoulder of hidden homosexuality (yes, I already knew by the age of five), a desire to shock, and the irresistibility of showing off. All three of these found a lifelong, I trust less obnoxious, release in front of the piano's black and white keyboard: life's lurid colours tamed, if never monochrome.

A writer is God: 'Let there be light.' A word is scrawled on the page and the world is changed. 'And the Word was made flesh' – an idea floating in the air is caught, a concept becomes carnal. The fox snaps closed his jaw.

## All things bright and beautiful

Thelwall School assemblies and the blond Danemann upright piano (my mother called this piano maker Danner-man for some reason) on which were thumped out hymns from the slender pink book. 'O Jesus I have promised' – the rush through the syllables of 'O Jesus' in the modern tune until the comforting rest on pro-*mised*. Mrs Stobbs. Our teacher. Her playing was vigorous and confident, like a baker thrashing loaves out of the morning's oven, flour on ample arms. She had a voice with a glint of a shriek in it. I remember her clapping her hands for silence in the classroom but not finding the sweet spot where air and palm crack, but rather dull bone and flesh which stings and barely sounds.

At Christmas my memories rise up again as I return to that childhood: 'Away in a Manger'. Mrs Stobbs's wrists dip and rise as she hammers out the F major chords over the kids' shrill singing. The homemade paper chains shake on the fir tree and the cotton wool hanging as silent snow or as the snagged beard of Santa Claus. This is a carol for children to sing but for adults to hear, unbroken voices belting through gaps in the milk teeth, memory frozen until that day (Adam's apple aching with nostalgia and tears barely held back) when our hearts melt and we hear the out-of-tune children's voices once more:

> *Be near me, Lord Jesus*
> *I ask you to stay*
> *Close by me forever*
> *And love me I pray*
> *Bless all the dear children*
> *In your tender cares*
> *And fit us for heaven*
> *To live with you there.*

My whole Thelwall childhood turns out to be a home-made Christmas card, a collage of Yuletide memories, a shining village of tinselled trees.

## Pulling up my socks

The playing field at Thelwall School had the school building on one side and gardens of houses backing on to it on the other three sides. So much grass – until it was time for us to play football, and then I wished for it be even larger. Large as the steppes of Russia; large as the outback scrub of South Australia. Large enough to swallow me up and prevent my mortification as the ball flew towards me and I was expected to kick it. 'Come on, Steve!' they screamed as the sphere sought me out like a target. It seemed preferable to me at that moment for it to be a grenade. I do remember exerting the fullest force on one occasion, pulling back my leg and exploding all my energy to the tip of my boot . . . and missing, falling into the mud accompanied by screams of derision and laughter from the other boys.

Then I discovered the perfect technique: socks. Whenever the ball seemed to be heading my way I would turn slightly and slowly start to pull up my socks . . . left . . . right. I would see the ball out of the corner of my eye as my calves were being covered, stretched tight with thick white poly-cotton. The ball would continue its approach and then . . . oh dear! *Just* too late to kick that match-winning goal or to dribble it forward and pass. The worst that could happen with my sock technique would be that the ball would hit me, full force. Usually it would pass me by, getting smaller as it flew towards one of the gardens at the edge and occasionally over the fence.

Later, at Chetham's, there was no football training that I remember, so my technique for avoiding sports had to change. I would simply 'forget' to bring my kit, the teacher would whack me on the backside with a sneaker as a punishment, then I could sit and read in the corner, sore seat, socks around my ankles.

## Circumcised

I glanced to the left in the urinal at Thelwall School. The good-looking boy. His penis looked different. 'He's Jewish,' whispered the other boy to me. In a school as white as a can of condensed milk this was exotic fruit indeed. There were no Africans, no Asians, no continental Europeans, just this one Jew and maybe one or two Catholics. But my father's maternal line apparently had Jewish ancestry, and he was circumcised – according to my mother, who should have known.

I myself never saw my father completely naked. At the swimming baths he would contort himself in the changing rooms, Houdini-like, writhing to avoid the tightly wrapped towel dislodging and revealing the member that made me. I saw his torso often as he sat cross-legged on the rug by the fire, shirt peeled off, massaged by my mother's best friend, Liz. Unmarried Liz, the midwife who delivered me and who lived in a flat near us when I was born. It was at her later flat in Airlie Road, Hoylake, that I heard Brailowsky's Chopin polonaises. She had the LP. I remember only the fumble in the dramatic central section of the A major one, op. 40 no. 1, an arthritic panic as he jumped down to the growling trills. A photo of a man with leather-beaten skin on the cover, as if a chain-smoker had never pursed his lips around the cigarette itself but rather had let the smoke from the smouldering tobacco whirl directly into his face. Later, backstage in the green room of the Philharmonic Society in Bilbao, I saw his photograph as a handsome young Jewish man. A glimmer of glamour and, one sensed, firmer trills.

Anyway, returning to that other circumcised man – my father. My mother told me later that when she was pregnant with me my paternal grandmother had said to her with some urgency, 'If it's a boy you *must* have him circumcised.'

My mother barely knew what that meant, then found out, then refused – and then my grandmother died before I was born. 'Your father was Jewish,' my mother said to me many years later. 'His family never accepted me because I was a Gentile.' I'm still trying to discover the connections here. Martha Marks was mentioned. But then Jane Marks appears in a genealogy chart. Giant's Hall farm in Wigan. The Gill family who married into the Marks family. But then there was the British Israelism connection. A cousin of mine told me that a travelling preacher from that sect, Rev. Jack Wintersgill, would often stay overnight at my father's family home, Highlands. This cleric was also a chaplain of the Orange Order. And lived in the next village to the Gills. Indeed, shared the Gill name. As do I. Sometimes the mists of time are welcome . . .

And so I never saw my father naked except . . . well, there was *that* occasion. In the long garden of All Saints Drive. It must have been a summer Sunday, deckchairs out, neighbours round, drinks on the lawn. My father was reclining with legs akimbo in his loose, khaki shorts, cradling a Pimm's or maybe a large gin and tonic. Conversation was lively, the dogs chasing after thrown balls, the sun blazing between light clouds. We were all sitting chatting and then . . . my father's legs spread and we all saw. He carried on talking but others' eyes were cast low. His penis was clearly visible through a gap in the leg of his baggy shorts. He wasn't wearing underwear, a kind of faddish thing he got into for a while. A sausage was on display. Our neighbours averted their eyes as my mother tried to catch his eye and gesture with her nose. 'Colin!' under her breath then a nod and a smile to the friends gathered. Nothing doing. His legs remained wide open, his dick blithely hanging for all to see. Then. One of our dogs, panting from exertion, lolloped over to him and, as he scratched her head affectionately, she leaned in and gave his dick a big lick. Like a flytrap his knees came together. Not until the neighbours had left was there mention of it and, I think, all was laughter. And yes . . . cut!

## Dogs

Taffy, Judy, Maggie, Flossy, Tristan and Isolde, Clive and Maud, Cyril, Maxico . . .

We always had dogs. My childhood memories are woven together with leashes on the banister, large tubs of Spillers Winalot, water dishes knocked over, smelly accidents on carpets, hair on clothes, wagging tails, tickling tummies.

The first dog, Taffy the corgi, I barely remember, but Judy the Border collie is as clear in my mind as a human friend from the time. She was a guard dog, a rounder-up, a sprinter. We were never close, as in romping on the floor with a squeaky toy. In fact she treated me like a ward, snapping at my heels if I strayed too far, nipping my buttocks on that occasion in Criccieth when I was frolicking in the sea on holiday.

Maggie, the Cavalier King Charles spaniel, was my first canine chum, and we were close, despite her bad breath. She was the first dog I was allowed to take out for a walk by myself. I must have been about nine by this time. Along the canal, down to the sweet shop, over to Winnie and Roger's. She looked up at me as if in encouragement: 'You're doing very well, I'm enjoying this!'

Flossy came along in my mid-teens, another corgi and a less complex character than Maggie – fresher breath, too. I'd call her in the garden: Flossss, relishing the combination of name and whistle which a sibilant 'S' allowed.

My mother became interested in the idea of obedience training (after her lost battle with me, perhaps) and two Alsatians joined our family: Tristan and Isolde. They both did well in shows, Isolde winning a minor prize at Crufts. Tristan was rather moody and highly strung (what else do you expect from a tenor?) but Isolde had that steady personality that responded well in the show ring. Many weekends my mother would bundle the dogs into the back of her Volvo at the crack of dawn and head off on the motorway to a show. The kitchen was littered with rosettes and a few hideous plastic trophies.

Clive and Maud were Italian greyhounds, doglets with spindly legs and narrow, shivery rib cages. Where Isolde would have walked over the Alps in a storm, Clive found a pee in the garden between the months of October and April a challenge. He would stand on the threshold, quivering with discomfort, looking back with pleading: 'Can't I just relieve myself on the carpet?' Sometimes he just did this without asking for permission. Both dogs would burrow under duvets and pillows, deeper, deeper until the airless embrace of down was like a womb. I learned never to sit down on a sofa or chair without poking around to see if a dog might be sleeping there.

Later was Cyril the Afghan, a breed that reminds me always of that occasion years later (I think it was in Florida) when an open-top sports car vroomed up to the traffic lights. A leather-jacketed man was driving, a glamorous blonde broad next to him in the passenger seat whose long hair shimmered in the breeze. Red light (wait) then green. The car turned the corner in a smooth curve and a snout came into view. The blonde woman was actually an Afghan bitch.

## Doris Cox and her knickers

My mother did a few jobs at one point to amplify her income and help pay for my piano lessons. In addition to being the lollipop lady at the Thelwall School crossing, she helped out at a local hen farm, did something called 'Welcome Wagon' when she called on families who had recently moved into the area to help acclimatise them to the neighbourhood, and had some job with the Prudential. Did she sell policies door to door? I can't think she did, but I do remember dear Doris Cox who did just that and who got my mother some extra work with the company. Doris was one of those Nescafé visitors to our house whom I loved to be around. She had tight curly blonde hair like Elisabeth Schwarzkopf and a bubbling laugh like a saucepan of milk about to rise and burn on the hob.

She always had fun stories to tell but I can't remember any of them – except something about her getting lost walking in a field with a friend. 'I laughed so much I wet my knickers,' she said, giggling uncontrollably and risking another accident. Every time we met I would remind her of it and her hilarity and mine would start all over again. The milk in the saucepan would rise and her blonde curls would shake. Fifty years later it's all that left of her in my memory, but somehow it's still something to treasure. A kind, lovely woman with an adorable sense of humour, a warm heart, and a pair of saturated knickers.

## Parents' bedroom

It's not just the fear of catching one's parents in the act of copulation that makes their bedrooms places of taboo. At least for me. It was a chamber of tears and fears and bitter words. I remember it always dark, curtains drawn, two narrow single beds separated by a bedside table (pills on my mother's side) with room for her friends to kneel in charismatic prayer when she had drawn the curtains of her soul – or, rather, thrashed behind them, blinded by a relapse of her nervous breakdown. An animal in fur-flying panic as her mind like meat minced out of control. I think I found the seraphic calm as the Bible was gently closed with a final 'Amen' (hallelujah!) more terrifying than the terror she had before. I couldn't think about it then, and I flinch to do so now.

My father read a lot but where were his books? There was a small, white bookcase opposite his bed sagging with oddments like a jumble sale's leftovers: Harold Robbins's *The Carpetbaggers*, next to a fat paperback called *Love in Action* (I googled it and there are multiple possibilities ranging from a lesbian love story to a book on Catholic social teaching). Then there was the fashionable-at-the-time *The Peter Principle* squashed next to John Fowles's *The Magus*, which in turn leaned heavily on Jacqueline Susann's *Valley of the Dolls*. Oh, and many of Erich von Däniken's UFO books. Fodder to buy at the airport gate before a long flight, for a family who never travelled. Warrington Public Library was where he went to fill his arms with books.

My father slept closest to the window, and I'm sure he always faced it as he lapsed into unconsciousness each night. I cannot gauge the depth of frustration he must have felt. Separate beds for separate souls. Under my father's bed (how did I discover?), between the mattress and the frame, squashed into creases, were a couple of porno magazines. Women in provocative poses not provoking me. One harder-core photo in one issue had a man lying naked next to the naked woman. That stirred something. In a wooden chest of drawers containing underwear, top drawer, pressed into the ancient dust of the grain, was one packet of Durex. I knew it was a contraceptive device but in my innocence I thought it must be a pill. One day, returning with heart beating fast to the drawer, I took it out again and rubbed it between my fingers where it squelched and squirmed. I'm pretty sure the sell-by date was from before I was born. Just think, if it had been torn open and used early in 1961 I may not exist.

## Pills and potions

Childhood maladies. Croupeline, Germolene, and then there was Composition Essence, my grandmother's cure-all: a spoonful of the sticky red liquid in a glass of hot milk, a pink promise of feeling better soon. I recently looked up the ingredients: lobelia herb, cayenne fruits, hemlock spruce, bayberry root bark, ginger root, clove buds, cinnamon bark, and oils of cassia, cajeput, peppermint, eucalyptus, pimento berry and clove bud. Something in that witch's brew has to have done the trick. Olbas Oil was another remedy in her arsenal. She would dab it on a pillow or on a hanky at the slightest suspicion of a blocked nose or a headache. Childhood insomnia or sickness smells like Olbas Oil to me.

My mother had a motorbike accident when she was about eighteen, tossed off the back as she rode along a Welsh country lane clutching her boyfriend. The doctor's 'You'll never walk again' changed into 'You'll never have children' which then, a decade later, changed into . . . me! The man responsible in part for this miraculous recovery was Mr Cotton, an osteopath and naturopath working in Liverpool. My grandfather must have known this pioneer somehow, and sent my mother to him. He then sent her to some sort of retreat or sanatorium, whence she emerged fully cured. She was a vegetarian for a while before

I was born, and then, latterly, a regular visitor to health-food shops, usually leaving with bursting bags of vitamins and supplements (there was always a tube of Redoxon in the kitchen next to the Roberts radio), from homeopathic tablets to sachets of fibre-rich constipation aids.

Later in life the cures became more chemical and they were for the unseen maladies of the mind – an array of tranquillisers and anti-depressants sleeping in bottles by her bedside. One pill she refused to take though, back in 1961, fighting terrible morning sickness, pregnant with me. 'I'm going to prescribe thalidomide for you, Mrs Hough. I think you'll find it will help,' said her doctor. Something told her not to follow his advice, and so I have arms and fingers with which to type these memories.

## Irby

A couple of times a year we would visit the home of two cousins of Auntie Liz: Margaret and Ethel Bell, sisters, spinsters. Thickest tweed skirts worn as armour, with helmets of permed white hair. Margaret's was a softer wave, more grey than white; Ethel's as fixed as a preacher's dogmas, frozen in place over a clean, pink scalp. Margaret was the outgoing one, slightly plumper, more openly friendly, more confidently hospitable. Ethel's shyness was painful – a hamster next to Margaret's tabby.

There is a middle-class, middle-aged, middle England 'look', and the Bells's bungalow seemed like a prime example, with its polished dining chairs, polished tiled fireplace, polished ornaments, polished brass doorknobs . . . everything shining and sparkling and kept-for-best. Their yellow dusters must have been threadbare. This tidied life in this immaculate bungalow was not so much post-post-war frugality (though there was that) but a sort of suburban, diminutive, doll's house Victoriana – the Empire's values and aspirations without the swagger and confidence that brought them to birth.

Nevertheless, all of this reflection came later. At the time I always enjoyed our visits to these unusual ladies, as no sooner were we seated in one of the winged chairs than Ethel would bring in trays of teacups alongside a china pot of dark, intensely flavoured tea, and a plate heavy with slabs of moist, sweet, homemade sponge cake. In the summer we would sit outside in their expansive garden with its massively thick hedge on every side – a tweed skirt of topiary. As a child it seemed to stretch all the way to Eden, a prelapsarian land of cakes and honey.

We could never visit on a Sunday because that was the Sabbath and, apart from attending church, they did nothing but read their Bibles and sing hymns around the polished fireplace. Ethel, the shyer one, had a voice as rich as fruit cake and she would warble 'Blessed Assurance, Jesus Is Mine' if she felt a rare burst of confidence. She had a vibrato that quavered like a bottle of lavender water on a shaky dressing table.

They were two women I find it impossible to imagine being married. They had an intense sibling intimacy, two cacti growing dustily in a hothouse, even if Margaret appeared to sit closer to the sun. Perhaps the latter might have allowed herself a whirlwind romance in a moment of madness; but never, like her cousin Liz, sharing a bed with my mother or giving my father a massage on the rug in front of the blazing log fire.

## Metal guru

There are so few musical memories of those early years. I know I was still practising the piano, and still going for lessons with Heather Slade, and still entering some local competitions, but there was no real interest in music beyond my assigned pieces. I could sing you the theme song to *Dad's Army* but had never heard any Puccini. Then I fell in love with pop music. It must have been around the early 1970s and it was probably sex. *Top of the Pops*, the BBC television show, had a weekly display of energetic young men, sweaty chests glistening, tight trousers thrusting (although I never fantasised about the bulge within), mouths sharing the bulbous mike-on-a-pole, joint spit in the foil, long hair tangled in duets of passion – my puberty was accompanied by the beat of drums and the twang of electric guitars.

Marc (oh, how wonderful the 'C', how grown up, how inaccessible) Bolan was the lead singer of T. Rex. I felt a lurch of sadness when the band's hit single 'Metal Guru' was displaced from the number 1 slot by Don McLean's 'Vincent'. I can visualise today the place when someone told me the

news in 1972. A straggly path from Thelwall County Primary past All Saints Church car park to All Saints Drive,
perhaps fourteen steps from the curb. A path of chewed-up
vegetation and a tatty wire fence. '"Vincent" is a better song,'
said my friend. He was right. I hear it today and it's good,
well sung, well written, touching. 'Metal Guru' is rusty and
drecky, perhaps one of the worst songs in a period with
many contenders. But Don McLean's homespun plucking
and farm boy features did nothing for my firing hormones.
Marc Bolan, his smile so naughty, so knowing, so cheeky, the
head tossed back, shirt open five buttons, tongue between
the teeth – he was the one on the glossy poster above my
bed, something stirring inside my chest as his image caught
sunlight from the window. 'Marc does not smoke tobacco.'
My father read that titbit in a newspaper interview with the
singer I'd left open. 'Means he smokes something else,' he
observed, with disapproval in his voice. He needn't have
worried. I never did. Well, one puff at the Ansonia Hotel ten
years later. One puff just to taste. Horrid burning leaves. No
further down than my tongue. 'Oh Debora, always look like
a zeb[o]ra.' Well, of course . . .

But glam and the boy-band beauties couldn't hold me
when I discovered Led Zeppelin. I didn't fancy Robert Plant
or any other of the sweat-stained, grungy progressives, but
the music went to a deeper place. I never felt the slightest
interest in joining that clan, the leather jackets, the greasy
hair, the beards, the tattoos, the drugs (thank God), but
those were the LPs I spent my pocket money on. *Keyboard*

*Giants of the Past* was in the past. I practised piano less and less, and cared about classical music less and less . . . until Elgar and Catholicism finally swept me away to a different planet, one from which I now observe (with affection and bemusement) that spotty youth in the Thelwall bedroom.

We cling to our tastes, our tastes are us, tongue-deep in the throat – while they last. Then we wake up and look in astonishment at our former fads. Who *was* that? A kid. The older me, mouth dry with embarrassment. It took *this* long?

## Beloved neighbours

When I was about nine years old Margaret and Philip Morey moved to All Saints Drive. One summer's day I heard the sound of a piano coming from their open window. I ran back to our house excitedly and burst in: 'Mum, Mum, the new neighbours play the piano!' I soon knocked on their door and so began a friendship that lasted without gaps for half a century. Margaret taught German at John Moores University in Liverpool, and Philip taught French at Manchester Metropolitan University. As Thelwall is equidistant from the two cities there was a neat symmetry as they travelled each morning in opposite directions from Warrington Central station. I was in their house numberless times over the years and we had plans in 2020 to meet for our usual Boxing Day dinner (they were fantastic cooks) until Covid-19 and then Margaret's death on that very day prevented it. They had no children but they were like parents to me, or perhaps elder siblings, or, even better, just wonderful friends.

In the early years I would give Margaret piano lessons in exchange for German lessons. I realise now, when playing in Germany or Austria, that she was the better student. The Moreys actually took me on my first trip abroad, to Düsseldorf – perhaps to practise my language skills? I ended up buying a hat instead, with a Bavarian brush pinned to the side. So many fun evenings were had at their home, sometimes with Philip singing Gilbert and Sullivan songs or with all of us gathered around the Scrabble board. These memories are all that's left now of my Thelwall years. And the tree outside our old house, cosy with compost.

# CHETHAM'S

# Naughty boy

Chetham's School has a long history, beginning as a college for the training of priests in the fifteenth century, then becoming a school for 'poor boys from honest families' in 1656, and finally the specialist music school it has been for over half a century. The original 1421 building survives as Chetham's Library where, in 1845, Karl Marx and Friedrich Engels met and sat and wrote, giving birth to the *Communist Manifesto*. Today the school is a place of serious study with a calm, confident vision of what it is trying, and succeeding, to do. It was not always thus.

It is impossible to write about Chetham's in the 1970s without criticism. To enter the school was to walk through the cobbled sandstone gatehouse, to the right of which were large metal bins where leftovers from lunch were deposited . . . to feed the pigs, we were told. Thus each day at Chets began with the reek of rotting food. By my second year most classes took place on a bomb site beyond those bins where prefabricated buildings perched, smelling of glue and sawdust, with squeaky doors and loose hinges and the creak of cheap, uncertain floors.

I began in the senior school in the autumn of 1972 and, to be frank, the place was a mess – physically, academically and (often) musically. My time there all but destroyed me and I left with a barely usable set of barely mediocre

O levels. The facilities at the school in those days were dire. The chemistry lab seemed as medieval as the library. I think there were five or six Bunsen burners, although not all of them worked. 'What are those crystals over there, sir?' We pointed at a spider's web obscuring the copperplate writing on the cloudy, dusty glass bottles. And then there were the practice rooms in Palatine House. One of them had such a large hole in the brick wall that it was literally possibly to climb through into the next room. The banisters on the stairwells leading up to those studios would, with a gentle pull, lift out of their sockets, exposing a three-floor drop down. Everything hung loose, let in draughts, wobbled, peeled, stuck. I don't believe in ghosts but this building seemed cursed with a terrible melancholy. It had originally been built in 1843 as one of the first railway hotels, servicing nearby Victoria station. Even as a schoolboy I could imagine its past, sad residents, alone in the small rooms, travelling salesmen staring hopelessly out of the sooted windows at the desolate industrial landscape.

Let me admit though, before going any further, that I was not blameless in my underachievement at Chetham's – and Marc Bolan might have had something to do with my distractions. I was often naughty in class and would sit at the back passing notes around, trying to make my fellow students laugh. I would frequently be sent out, along to the headmaster's office in disgrace. I would ask outrageous questions or offer outrageous subjects for discussion. I remember tracing the word WOW on the chalkboard with the point of a compass. Little did I realise that when the board would next be dusted clean of the 'causes of the French Revolution' that 1970s word of exclamation would shout out with a chalky white splendour. 'Who did this?' demanded the teacher. Well, at least I owned up. Sent out once more.

## Random teachers

I was at Chetham's during its most dysfunctional and (as we now realise) criminal period. Although there were some very good teachers (Ian Little, Trevor Donald, John Leech, Robert MacFarlane, Michael Asquith spring to mind), most of them seemed to have come from some catalogue of misfits, eccentrics and (I will no longer be hit over the head for saying so) sadists.

Mr Raby was the deputy head who also taught maths – often with one of his basset hounds (Hugo or Humphrey) lying on top of the desk in front of him licking its genitalia. He had a strange walk with a bobbing upper-body movement like some giant, tweed-jacketed pigeon – always a pipe leaving clouds of smoke in his trail, always dressed in tobacco-brown clothes. Once, when I fell down the stairs (I was seeing if I could hop down on one leg – I couldn't), he took me into his office and I saw a kindness in him that I'd never seen before. He made me a mug of tea to overcome the shock and forced me to drink it with lots of sugar: 'You're having a cup of tea whether you like it or not,' he said with a brown-toothed smile.

Mrs Jones taught us General Studies. She was a kind, caring soul but we made terrible fun of her, pushing the envelope to the edge. I did a project on James Joyce's *Ulysses* once, reading out my essay in front of the class as a short presentation. I'd chosen the fruitier passages, planning to declaim about the 'scrotumtightening sea', but I got no further than 'James Joyce was born in . . .' before being reduced to hysterical laughter. I made about four attempts without making it to Dublin, each time more helpless, and Mrs Jones, in a rare moment of anger, told me to sit down. Just as well, as I hadn't even read the book – and still haven't to this day. And I avoid swimming in the sea at all costs.

Ian Little was my English teacher for most of the five years I spent at Chets. I remember illuminating classes on *The Crucible* and *A Kestrel for a Knave* (though why did we spend so much time on such a thin book?), but above all I was conscious that he was on my side with patience and high marks when I occasionally pushed outrageousness to the limits. Once we were given a random word to write an essay on – mine was 'bacon'. I went into sixth gear on a roller-coaster of smashed-up grammar with a surging cross-current stream of consciousness ('it is pink yes it is pink slice it up my bacon just sit on the rasher'). I don't think my piece was very good but somehow he sensed there was a sizzle there worth encouraging.

I still remember the haiku lesson when he stood with a piece of chalk in his hand, silent, thinking for quite a number of seconds, then wrote out the following:

*A haiku consists*
*Of five, seven and of five:*
*Of what, I wonder?*

Stanley Jones was my first teacher there, before I was moved up a year to first-form senior school. He was musically inclined and gentle, always smelling of Pears soap. He had a strange nervous laugh that would suddenly engulf him and made him seem sad – it was an explosive guffaw that switched on, and then off. Much later I knew him as a bitter, tragic old man, refusing visits except occasionally from young men he'd met who would come to give him massages. He was always very kind to me, though, and before his decline he was a frequent visitor to our house. He's the unnamed person in my book *Rough Ideas* who told me my playing was 'dreadful' but who, in so doing, changed the direction of my pianistic life. He'd invite boys over to his house in Didsbury for a 'Guinness and cheese' lunch. It sounded like a euphemism but actually, on the one occasion I went, he did just offer me food and drink. He'd put Delius on the record player and as the sonorous harmonies would swamp his musty study his eyes would fill with tears. He was a man of great sensitivity who never seemed to have found a healthy way to express it.

Donald Clarke taught a number of subjects, including the piano, but in the one sex education class I remember him taking he was unable to face talking about the human body. I still remember his awkwardness, his fidgeting, his cracking voice, his blushing cheeks. He couldn't have been more embarrassed if he'd been acting out the sexual intercourse he was trying to describe instead of talking about it. Somehow I remember a ferocious temper too, very rarely displayed but terrifying when it was.

Another teacher taught another subject – I will leave the details vague as it is neither helpful nor pleasurable to say more. 'You're useless. You'll do nothing with your life,' he once screamed at me as he strode to the back of the classroom to strike me forcefully across the head, as if to make sure my brain would not have the capacity to contradict him. He was a pitiful character, tall and gawky with no self-control. One occasion was quite horrifying. The class was making fun of him yet again and somehow things got out of hand. At the high point of the commotion he let out an immense roar: 'Will you just STOP it!' On the word 'stop' he flung his hand up into the air in emphasis and hit it with tremendous force against a light fitting, his roar of anger turning into a roar of pain. The class erupted in laughter and he burst into tears, a total wreck of a man. Children will always be cruel, but for a teacher self-control comes before crowd control. An ability to laugh at himself, to deflate the situation by a change of mood, to turn things around, a light touch . . . he had none of them and suffered (how he must have suffered!) as a result.

Penry Williams, our history teacher, was wiser. He was also subject to some teasing (he had a lisp, a light covering of wispy blond hair and a limping leg – he would frequently trip over someone's briefcase or a chair or a desk) but as he seemed to be oblivious, so the teasing ceased. One lunch-time, inspired by the recent exhibition at the Tate Gallery of Carl Andre's *Equivalent VIII* (the infamous pile of bricks), I decided to create my own version . . . on the teacher's desk. I hauled inside the classroom a great pile of filthy bricks from the damp dump outside (some of them crawling with worms, all of them encrusted with dank soil) and assembled them on his desk in a great, scratching, dirty row. We waited in anticipation for Penry to return from lunch. He opened the door and limped in and immediately saw the installa-tion. He stood in front of it for a few seconds and smiled. 'Very interesting, very inventive. Now whose idea was this?' I owned up and he smiled again, not exactly a beam but a gentle 'assessing the situation' grin. 'Now you can remove them before we begin the class.' No punishment or fuss. For years later he would mention these bricks to me and would tell people about them after I had begun my career as a pian-ist. ('Those bricks, Stephen. They showed a certain . . . what shall I say, creative impulse.') Even though I remember little of the lessons he was a wise old bird on matters of human nature and child psychology.

Michael Brewer was head of music but he also taught me composition for a year. I was his first lesson of the day at nine o'clock and I remember him always arriving a little late and rather bleary-eyed. He was an excellent teacher, though, and had that sort of enthusiastic encouragement which made me want to go out of the lesson and write more music (the most important quality in a teacher). He performed a song I'd written to words of Christopher Logue: 'Friday, Wet Dusk'. I much enjoyed setting the word 'mastication' and enjoyed even more my teacher being forced to sing it in public.

I also began an opera, with a libretto by my father: *Adam and Eve*. The two leading characters were to be (of course) naked on stage and the words 'My world, this is my world', to be sung by Adam, sounded, Mike said, like they should be sung by Harry Secombe, the large-voiced, large-stomached tenor most famous for being one of the characters in *The Goon Show*. Not a compliment, I feared. Like Mozart I began writing in full orchestral score; unlike Mozart I ran out of inspiration by page 5 or so. Not 'my world' at that moment . . . although Dad's libretto was pretty extensive. I wonder where it is now?

Brewer also conducted us in the school orchestra. I have the LP to this day: *Belshazzar's Feast* by Walton. In blue ink on the back of the sleeve I wrote, 'On this recording I played xylophone, tambourine, castanets, anvil, glockenspiel.' One of the most terrifying times I ever had on stage was with Brewer conducting the Tenth Symphony of Shostakovich. I was playing the extremely exposed, extremely tricky side-drum part and I got the second movement entry wrong in every rehearsal. In the concert he gave me a cue of terrifying ferocity and clarity. It worked. The offbeat figure was fired off like a pistol direct to the heart.

After Michael Brewer I went for composition lessons to Neil Garland, who was also a clarinettist. Studies with Neil were more systematic and I learned a lot. He asked me to write a clarinet quartet (three B flat clarinets and bass clarinet) for his ensemble in Huddersfield which they performed in 1976. He had an unusual beard, like Wagner's, growing only from the jawline down. Again, I always left his lessons wanting to sharpen my pencils.

Of course, reluctantly, I can't leave it there. I had no idea at the time that some of the teachers at Chetham's were sexual predators and were grooming and abusing under-age girls at the school. Indeed, some ended up later with prison sentences. The school has weathered immense storms over these issues and has not only survived that era but has truly been reborn, triumphing over the earlier dysfunctions with energy and excellence. It wouldn't be fair to the victims not to mention the negative past, but it's a joy to be able to celebrate the present, and a credit to the school to have achieved such a complete recovery.

## Shit in a bottle

*A row of kids.*
*Chlorine spandex.*
*Shrivelled.*
*Don't get an erection.*
*Shivering in a line.*
*Spindle-legs.*
*Milkshake-straw legs.*
*Thin veins.*
*Hairless.*

*Giggles besides the scum-dreg rim.*
*Pre-dived blue liquid.*
*Flat blue. Plate.*
*Skim-smooth as a teenager's stomach.*

We're standing at the deep end. Everyone is talking loudly. Body language is tough and nervy, coiled, greyhound in the slips. The echoes of kids' chatter ricochet off the tiled walls and the reflected dank floor, its clammy verruca pools stirred with grey grime. The boys are, one by one, leaping into the water. I'm standing trembling in my trunks.

'Let's 'ave a bit o' quiet 'ere, lads.' Voice bully-booming over the half-broken-voiced, childish screams. He looks at me: 'Get in the water. 'Urry up!'

Who was this man? Not our usual sports teacher, whose punishment when I forgot my kit (on purpose) was a whack on the backside with a tennis shoe.

'I can't swim, Sir . . .'

My throat is stiff with fear – of the water and the teasing. He doesn't hear me though, and the others' splashing, jumping, slicing up out of the bracing froth, I hope, is a distraction. But not for long.

'*Get into the water, lad!*' he barks.

'I can't swim, Sir.'

Faces in the pool below me like sharks pushed and pulled under/over the sloshing surface, thrust down then breast-stroked in exuberant motion. Joy in water. Fluent as fish.

'Nonsense! Course ya bloody can! Jump in!'

His rough hand follows his rough words and, slipping on the side of the pool, I hear the laughter a second before I am pushed into the water, face first, ears under, deaf to the derision. Panic thrashing, body falling to floor. How to float? Flailing and flushed crimson I beat a track to the side and grasp the rusting rail, spitting out water, spraying water, kicking the deep water in complete humiliation. Gasping. Nose stinging. Heaving. Harrowing. Kids' shouting all echoes in the rectangular, white-tiled chamber.

This teacher was a tough man. You didn't mess with him. There was a back-slapping mateyness on the surface but underneath I sensed a coiled spring, a Rottweiler with no muzzle. Wasn't sure whether to share this. Best keep these things bottled up inside. Or just let them float away . . . shit in a bottle.

## Cecilia Vajda inside our bones

In my first year at Chetham's we were taught ear training by an extraordinary woman, Cecilia Vajda. She brought to Manchester from Budapest the Zoltán Kodály method, thrilling and terrifying us in equal measure. She had a fiery intensity, an infectious vivacity, the sharpest ear, a passion for music and for teaching it, and an absolute intolerance for the slightest nonsense or fooling around. Our fear quickly morphed into respect as we heard the results she was able to get from these ten- and eleven-year olds: sloppy rhythm tightened, uncertain pitch tuned, flabby phrasing focused.

She handed out scores of Britten's *Missa Brevis* and we began with the Gloria, but only the rhythm. This movement is in a lopsided, swinging 7/8 and until we had this beat snapping its fingers inside our very bones we could not continue. It was like discovering a muscle until then unused, and it was exhilarating. Then she left the school, and she left a gap no one has ever quite filled.

## Latin and the greenhouse effect

The lessons took place in a makeshift greenhouse, even though not a trace of green could be detected amidst the withering plants and desiccated twigs. This was the option at Chetham's if a pupil wanted to study Latin – a dry subject in a dusty room. The teacher, Mr Charles Lansome, was a strange, gnome-like man: short, bald, completely toothless, his mouth empty of dentures, with a massive nose like the bulb of one of the cactus plants gasping for life on the rickety shelves. He was actually retired but the school brought him in whenever a teacher was ill. He taught just about every subject (he was probably a fascinating person to talk to), but only *he* taught Latin. As twelve- or thirteen-year-olds we made fun of him mercilessly. He was gentle and kind, but those qualities do not count much to spotty pubescent boys with youthful talons eager to taunt. Such cruelty only reveals its ugly face with time . . . and experience and our own woundings.

As someone who did as little work as possible at school, and whose grades showed it, I was not going to take such unappetising, non-obligatory classes. The only Latin I learned was the text of the Mass when we studied and sang Benjamin Britten's *Missa Brevis*, and the famous phrase 'Dulce et decorum est pro patria mori' – Horace reworked by Wilfred Owen who was one of the set poets for O-level English.

I don't feel so guilty any more about my lousy school grades, but I do feel shame about dear old Mr Lansome in his greenhouse. Perhaps all those plant pots needed was a little water.

## Isador

At some point at Chetham's I was assigned for chamber music lessons with an American visitor, Michael Isador. I was tremendously taken with Mr Isador, his nonchalant confidence, the nasal accent (I think he was the first American I'd met), the jeans worn as a fashion statement, his immaculate black turtleneck sweater. In my world jeans were for digging in the garden but here was someone who wore them suavely. They looked perfectly worn and perfectly washed. Going back on the bus to Cheshire to catch the latest episode of *Crossroads* . . . well, it didn't seem a fit somehow. Benny, the fictional motel's handyman, would have worn jeans but they would have been baggy and rough and paint-stained. Mr Isador's pale blue-rinsed pair were from a different universe, not just a different continent.

He was sarcastic and tough and his comments often stung, but I loved my lessons . . . and he was obviously right. How could such an elegantly rolled neck not support a head containing a brain of wisdom and knowledge? We played Beethoven's C minor Trio op. 1 no. 3. I so wanted Mr Isador to like my playing but he didn't seem very impressed. How did the school get someone so distinguished to descend to the basement of Palatine House to teach TV-watchers like me? He'd studied at Juilliard. With Rosina Lhévinne. I was dazzled. 'Goodness! Was she wonderful?' I knew her from my *Keyboard Giants of the Past* LP, playing the Mozart Two-Piano Sonata with her husband Josef – another world, another continent. 'No, not really.' Wow. I was even more impressed. How could someone who had studied with this legend not love her? Mr Isador rose higher still in my estimation.

He worked a lot with the Hungarian violinist György Pauk and he told us of a concert he was playing with him the following week. 'Wow, what repertoire, Mr Isador?' 'We're doing Grieg C minor.' 'Gosh, there are some tricky things in there, aren't there!' 'No, not really.' Oh, Mr Isador really was the thing. I wanted to study solo piano with him. I could stop watching the soaps and stop eating Findus Crispy Pancakes and could go to America where they really knew what's what and the burgers were rare and all was sophisticated and jeans were trendy and sweaters hugged flat stomachs, and I could have a nice day and grab a coffee with cream to go. How provincial our Nescafé at home seemed, with its instant granules and boiled milk. His coffee of choice would probably have been an espresso. Gosh, what's that? So small? A puddle at the bottom of one of our ceramic, Masonic mugs.

## Steele more

Douglas Steele was one of the greatest musicians I've ever met. Every gesture, every word of his, breathed music, its vibrations and the wordless stories then told through the sounds. Every line when he played had the grace of a dancer, gravity and flight in perfect union. He was, though, by the time he taught me and increasingly so as he changed from tutor to friend, quite mad, always straddling the faultline between eccentricity and insanity.

'Get in the corner, boy.' He flung his hand towards one of the pock-marked, paint-peeling walls of the Victorian teaching studio of Palatine House. He'd been assigned to teach me composition when I was twelve years old. 'What chord is this?' He flung his hand now on to the keys, creating a clangorous jangle of a chord on the out-of-tune, blond, Danemann upright. 'Sing the middle note,' he cried, with barely time for me to hear the harmony before another chord was struck. Yet somehow, as this manic progression continued, and I was gasping for breath, I was learning. I was hearing the DNA of chords, how wonderful their variety, how they ring in the ear: the fingerprints of harmony.

Then every week he would at some point in the lesson play the beginning of Debussy's 'Hommage à Rameau', with a rapturous sense of narrative and improvisation, turning to me (every week) at bar nine: 'Michelangeli keeps the pedal on here.' I knew it was coming every week as the lesson progressed, that plain, plaintive opening in G sharp minor, as if a duet for cor anglais and bassoon, a plangent, lonely phrase. Bar eight would arrive and then . . . I knew it was coming: 'Michelangeli keeps the pedal on here.' Somehow it always seemed a revelation, something daring and intoxicating as Douglas disobeyed the marking in the score in homage to the great Italian pianist. The D sharp major chord hung in the air, defying the laws of score-reading and the sound-board's speed of evaporation. The chord is still ringing as I remember it today.

In later years, long after I graduated from the Royal Northern College, I would meet up with him at his house in Didsbury. 'Burglars go away!' he'd written on a piece of paper displayed in his front window. 'Watch your step, don't trip,' he'd affixed to the stairs as you'd climb to the upper floor to visit the loo. Of course, I almost did trip, my foot trying to avoid the loose paper sheet as my mind bent around the craziness of the warning. Once, after a delicious curry in Rush-olme, we returned to his house for coffee and he sat down at the piano to play me a couple of new pieces he'd written. 'Oh they're lovely, Douglas!' I exclaimed. And he always played the piano so beautifully, with such warmth. Then later in the evening he took out a volume of pieces by William Baines. 'You should play his music. Totally under-appreciated. Died young. Genius.' He then proceeded to play some of Baines's Preludes. Two of them were . . . yes! The very same pieces he'd played for me earlier as his own compositions, written out with his own shaky hand. 'Oh they're lovely, Douglas!' seemed to be the only possible response.

He was a damaged man, shell-shocked during the Second World War not by facing fire in the line of battle but because he had made a mistake as a radar operator and a plane had been shot down. He never recovered from this trauma and, despite pre-war experiences as an assistant to Bruno Walter and Sir Thomas Beecham, what had been a promising career fizzled out. And, like so many men in the late 1940s, he just didn't fit in with the post-war world. He taught at Stockport Grammar School, creating a battalion of disciples who still to this day stand to attention at the mention of his name; he played the organ at a local church; he accompanied voice lessons at Chetham's; and he taught me composition . . . but somehow all was sadness and wasted talent. 'Watch your step, don't trip!' It was too late for Douglas.

## The wise man with the pipe

Gordon Green. Just to write his name fills me with a mixture of affection and gratitude – and I see him clearly before my eyes. Or rather I see smoke before my eyes, behind which a kind, wise face is just discernible through the mist. Encircling the pipe is a white goatee and, above, steel-rimmed spectacles are perched in front of energetic eyes. His smile was false, as in flashed from dentures which would shift precariously when clenching his pipe, but from the smiling eyes I never knew a more genuinely warm man.

Gordon was teaching Heather when Heather was teaching me and he'd heard me in some local competitions, including the National Junior Piano Playing Competition. At a certain point Heather wanted him to give me regular lessons so we went to meet him at his house in Liverpool – 33 Hope Street, equidistant from the two cathedrals. 'I don't teach children,' he told us, but he made an exception, requesting that I should continue seeing Heather but have my main lessons with him on Saturdays at his house. He also asked that one of my parents sit in on these lessons, to make notes, and to remind him that he was teaching someone inexperienced and immature. So my father came along each week, adding more smoke to the high-ceilinged room as they both puffed away on their pipes. When the lessons were over Gordon's wife, Dorothy, would come into the room with a tray on which were mugs of good coffee and Jacob's Club Plain biscuits. To think of those thick, plain-chocolate bricks under the green sleeve is to be placed instantly in his studio in 1973, and to smell once again Gordon's tobacco – Gold Block. It came in a tin and I can still hear the click as the lid snapped shut.

Those Saturday mornings were probably the highlight of my musical education. I'd lived in a musical bungalow until then, and now I was being given a guided tour of Versailles. One day Gordon had been listening to Alfred Cortot before we arrived and as we entered the room he said to me: 'My dear boy, just listen to this.' He dropped the needle on the LP and we heard the Chopin Etude op. 25 no. 1, nicknamed the 'Aeolian Harp'. In the final thirty seconds of the piece he turned to me and beamed. 'Listen to how Cortot shades the pedal to create that shimmering effect.' It was like a breeze through the window and it was the beginning of his incessant insistence on taking care with the pedal. There was not one lesson I had with Gordon when he hadn't something to say about its use. 'The soul of the piano', said Anton Rubinstein. One might also say the blood in the veins. Without pedal the piano is lifeless, desiccated, a shell.

In his music room (second door along on the right after entering the thick, Georgian front door) were two grand pianos, a brown Steinway and a black Bechstein, both old and worn. 'I prefer working on the Bechstein because it has more room to put my pencils,' he said. I never quite understood that, especially as he used one blue Staedtler clutch pencil with its thick lead, kept in the pocket of his fisherman's smock. But for someone whose obsession with sound and pedalling was so intense and constant it was surprising that these two instruments were so ungrateful to play. The old Bechstein had a kind of thin, grey sound which many of the less good instruments from that house can have. But that Steinway. It was truly one of the most unpleasant instruments: heavy action, uneven voicing, strangled sound. Or was that the point? If you could make this ugly machine sound good you wouldn't fear any concert piano.

Gordon kept me on a low-calorie diet (beginning with Mozart's Sonata K332 and Chopin's Nocturne in B major op. 32 no. 1) with great attention to detail, nothing left astray, nothing unsung, yet never a feeling of fussiness, and no pretence or showing off. Everything honest, natural. 'My ideal pianist is someone who knows the score inside out and is concerned about every aspect of notation and historical performance practice, yet can still play with the freedom and imagination of a Paderewski' – the pianist who had moved him in concert more than any other. Sir Clifford Curzon, a friend of his, apparently had the same reaction to the Polish pianist. Gordon's liberal spirit and lack of pedantry was a wonderful foundation for me, although his frequent lack of concern with accuracy or some technical specifics later meant that I had to work extremely hard when I studied with Derrick Wyndham after Gordon became too ill to teach. But maybe Gordon's lack of focus in my mid-teens actually saved me. Like my parents he let the boat float along when I'd lost my compass, with a gentle push or holding from time to time, an eye on the bigger waves, but no shaking out of a map with a demand to know every minute in which direction I was drifting.

'I don't care how you play now. It's how you're going to play in ten years that interests me' – no artificial grooming, no fakery, no hurried polishing for competitions. There was probably no word that was more anathema to him than 'competition'. Of course he saw their usefulness when the time was right, but that a student in the early stages of formation would already have competing as the main goal would have drawn from him a withering comment. It's not that doing competitions is ill advised, or that they are inherently evil, but obsessing about them can fetter the imagination at the very point in one's education when the imagination should be running riot. Instead he encouraged limitless experimentation, the freedom to take dead-end paths, with a total lack of concern about which piece would impress the jury, or which way of playing that piece would impress the jury. To start too early on the competition route is to cash in the investment before it's had time to gain any interest; it's picking fruit from the tree before it's ripened. 'In practice a perfectionist, in performance a realist' is another saying of Gordon's which can liberate as well as make demands, and about which I've written before. But one could turn that bon mot around: for the immature competition entrant, 'in practice a realist, in Round One a perfectionist', a warped way of thinking for someone who wants music to be their lifelong vocation.

One regret with Gordon was that he would never play for us. He was afraid that demonstration would result in imitation. If he asked for something, rather than show me he would say, 'Now just *think* for a few seconds. Hear what you want to do, then try it.' I respect the mental discipline behind this, but in my own teaching a point made at the keyboard isn't so much a template to be copied as a description in sound; the more talented students will take what you suggest and make it their own. Gordon had been a performer paralysed with nerves in his youth and it's possible that, no longer being in shape, he felt more able to describe what he wanted in words than to show it with fingers. He made the point once that a teacher who played the piano effortlessly was often not the best equipped to help someone who was having difficulties.

He died when I was about seventeen. In the last months of his life, after his beloved wife Dorothy's recent death, when he was lying on a sort of sofa bed in North Villas, Camden (he'd moved to London a few years before), he said to me in a weakened voice behind wheezes of catarrh, 'I'd like you to call me Gordon now, not Mr Green.' I was never quite able to make the switch before he died and I deeply regret that there was no time for me to change from student to friend. Lung cancer. All that wisdom, all that humanity, disappeared, gone in a puff of smoke.

## Can I learn some passionate Chopin?

Gordon wanted me to learn slowly, carefully. With a student who has fast fingers and a certain natural flair there is no problem rattling through the Grieg Concerto, or taking a Liszt Hungarian Rhapsody by the scruff of the neck, fur and felt flying . . . but no. When I began lessons with him aged ten he gave me that elegant Mozart sonata and that demure Chopin nocturne. Even though I knew my playing was improving under his guidance I was chomping at the bit, straining at the leash. I wanted to play something more headstrong, more dramatic. 'Mr Green, can I learn some passionate Chopin?'

The piece I had in mind was the Third Scherzo. I'd heard it on an LP we'd bought of Gordon's most famous student at the time, John Ogdon. This was the turbulence I craved: the mysterious, harmonically unhinged shiftiness at the beginning; the tumbling into the main theme's fiery octaves, blazing in both hands; the central section's warm repose; the coda's terrifying, passionate dash to the edge of the cliff. It's one of Chopin's most tightly constructed and authoritative pieces. Scherzo? My dictionary said the term meant 'a joke'. Where was this to be found in the bare-boned strides of the assertive main theme? Then the sublime major chorale . . . ah, yes! That must be the joke: the chords the punchline, the cascading arpeggios the laughing response. I must have been joking.

Gordon had been right. I was not really ready for such a piece but still, he let me learn it. I banged through the octaves and faked the rippling arpeggios. The coda where turbulence becomes a tornado – I jammed the pedal down, my twelve-year-old torso writhing (do I look passionate?), final octave scissor, head flung in the air, and the last, emphatic, defiant C sharp major chords. But instead of the final held unison in the bass I played a sort of drumroll effect: BRRRRRUM. Short and sharp. Hands flung from the keyboard. I could hear the applause of two thousand people in the audience. Up from the bench with a smile, arms flung outwards to embrace my fans, major career begun, managers fighting to sign me, and a record contract in the bag. 'Stephen, that was the most tasteless thing I've ever heard. You sound like a pub pianist.' Gordon's cutting words (rare from him), and I was transported from Carnegie Hall in New York to the Pickering Arms in Thelwall on quiz night. 'Play us some songs from the shows, Steve!' 'Climb Every Mountain', perhaps? I had more to learn in Hope Street than playing the piano.

## Philharmonic Hall and three piano recitals

After my Saturday piano lessons, firstly with Heather in Hoylake and later with Gordon in Liverpool, we would often attend concerts at Philharmonic Hall, either with the orchestra or piano recitals on the main stage. Hope Street, running from cathedral to cathedral, from cutting-glass-edged 1960s Catholic to fairytale neo-Gothic Anglican . . . bang in the middle, geographically, chronologically and stylistically, is the 1939 art deco (Streamline Moderne) concert hall, home of the Royal Liverpool Philharmonic Orchestra.

Three piano recitals attended in my youth remain in my memory and made a huge impression. Firstly, Sviatoslav Richter. The glamour of Russian artists in those pre-glasnost days was palpable even to a news-ignorant kid from Cheshire, and backstage (I tried unsuccessfully to get an autograph) bristled with heavy-set Russian men looking impatient and cruel and smelling of sweat and nicotine. Or am I projecting backwards? I don't remember details about the playing but I remember being transfixed – not least by the encores. I'm sure he gave at least five. It's the only time I heard Richter live. He's not a pianist I'm automatically drawn to now on recordings (there are important exceptions) but I tingle to this day with the memory of the electricity he created on that evening. It was an early lesson that, in the right hands, a plain, straightforward, gimmick-free piano recital could be a theatrical event of monumental impact.

I've mentioned that John Ogdon studied with Gordon

Green, so when we attended the former's afternoon recital at the Phil in the mid-1970s it seemed especially exciting. 'Do you think I will ever play on that stage?' I asked my mother. We proudly sat close to Gordon in the stalls so I, for a couple of hours, felt part of this magical but otherwise inaccessible adult world of concert life. John Ogdon was a name I'd heard often on Gordon's lips and I remember seeing a score on his desk of the Busoni Concerto with annotations by Gordon's teacher (and Busoni's student) Egon Petri. John was coming in later that day for a lesson on that monumental work. That afternoon at his recital Ogdon spun *pianissimos* that amazed and entranced me (how could a piano sound so feather light? How could such a large man play so quietly?) and I went up to my teacher at the end: 'Oh, Mr Green, wasn't it wonderful!' 'It's a pale shadow, my boy, of what he can do. He is a sick man and his playing reflects that. Everything so fast and helter-skelter. I am deeply disappointed.' I was deeply puzzled but didn't know then that Ogdon was suffering from severe mental illness, drugged and depressed. He was a pianistic genius who was now turning the corners of his concerts on one wheel. We headed backstage to meet the enormous pianist and Gordon introduced me as one of his pupils. John bent down to me kindly with a warm smile. 'It's very nice to meet you, Stephen. So what are you learning at the moment?' I'd brought an LP for him to sign, which he did with chubby fingers almost the circumference of my wrists. I still have it.

Then later I heard Alfred Brendel and it was a *musical* discovery more than a pianistic one. Three sonatas: Schubert

G major, Beethoven op. 109 and 110. I had played the latter sonata but never even heard the Schubert and it was like seeing a vast landscape for the first time. Until then I tended to like pieces which I could grasp in my hands, my brain, my emotions, but here was music that somehow eluded the imprisonment of possession, music that was free because it flew so high, music suggesting answers to questions unasked. That glorious Schubert sonata, opening in utter peace before clouds gather; except in this sunniest of his great sonatas it's only ever a summer's day darkening. Something in the serenity of those first bars, their stillness emphasised not disturbed by the nudging upbeats; and Brendel's focus, his uncompromising attention to this piece's inner life and sublimity . . . I felt like it was a musical coming of age on the spot. I crossed a threshold that evening, and it wasn't just the art deco arch of Philharmonic Hall, Liverpool.

## Not Paderewski

At the end of my earliest attempts at composition (mostly scribbles to fill space much as someone might say words, regardless of their meaning, to fill silence) I would sign: Frederic Chopin. That name was the symbol of all I wanted to be at the piano. His was the music which, to that nine-year-old, inserted the point of its dart most deeply. I could sing Chopin's melodies, even with imagination alone, and make my eyes water. And the scores I bought were the Polish edition. The so-called Paderewski edition.

This great pianist and former prime minister of Poland was probably involved in the editorial process merely to the point of allowing his name to appear on the cover (and few people in the late 1960s would have known or taken his piano playing seriously anyway), but he was still a symbol of authority and authenticity. My *Guinness Book of Records* listed him as the highest-paid performer in history, earning an estimated $10 million by the time of his death in 1941. As mentioned earlier, he was on my beloved *Keyboard Giants of the Past* LP, and I knew something about him too from Harold Schonberg's *The Great Pianists*, even though that book seems more concerned with emphasising his pianistic deficiencies than trying to understand why some, like Gordon Green, had spoken of him as the most mesmeric performer they'd ever heard. William Mason, the American student of Liszt, tried to put his finger on what it was in Paderewski's playing that appealed to such vast crowds: 'It possesses that subtle quality expressed in some measure by the German word *Sehnsucht*, and in English as "intensity of aspiration".'

But back to my scores. Their covers were almost the colour of my hand, and, unlike my hand, slightly oversized. My first purchase was the mazurkas, music I played in the National Junior Piano Playing competition mentioned earlier. By the time I was playing the ballades and scherzos there had been a reprint and the volumes had shrunk to standard size but the design and colour were kept – as was Paderewski's name. The Communist-era paper was rough and cheap, and after a few weeks of practising it looked tatty. If a marking near the stave were to be erased the notes would disappear too and, if rubbed too vigorously, the paper itself would form a hole, dust on the music desk of the piano. But this crumbling also made them seem like scores with which one had lovingly spent time. The patina of practice. The wear and tear of study. I learned only two mazurkas from my copy but it looked like I'd spent a life-time playing all of them. The spine cracked and had to be held together with tape, the cover was soon blotched and stained, the pages were roughed up.

And the stains? Orange juice. My mother used to pack me a lunchbox in the mornings and, along with tongue sand-wiches on springy sliced white bread with some Branston pickle bumping the surface, there would be a Tupperware container of juice. I carried my lunch in a capacious black briefcase with a one-slot clasp and a hard leather handle that swivelled and chafed, my palm creased with welts and the handle scabbed with sweat. The plastic bottle was squashed into the side and as the day pressed on the leather sides would press in, often resulting in a leaky bottle. I have many music scores to this day blotched with orange juice.

But there was another defacement. Some of those scores from that time are inscribed with my name. Every twenty pages or so my mother, in her not-neat curled handwriting, would scrawl 'Stephen Hough' in blue felt-tip – to avoid them being stolen, I suppose. With the cheap Paderewski paper this would bleed through to the next page. And worse. She sometimes, for protection's sake, would stick vinyl wallpaper on the outside of the scores – she'd found a roll somewhere with a swirling purple, pink and turquoise pattern. Thank goodness she ran out of energy (or wallpaper) after a few attempts, but Liszt's Hungarian Rhapsodies nos 9–15, Schirmer edition, sit on my library shelves to this day, perfectly preserved, a distant garish scream from the 1970s.

## No witnesses

I was terrified of trains: not being hit by one but being hit *on* one. To be stuck in a carriage, no way to get off between stations, no one to help in an emergency – this was a nightmare for me as a boy. Did I really think at rush hour I'd be alone in there, bait for the muggers? Phobias have no logic. The easiest way to get from Thelwall to Manchester was on the train; the only other way was on a bus, which involved being dropped off at the terminus of the number 3 in Flixton, ten miles away. So that's what we did, for five years. It was often a race to the line as we hurtled along in the car from Thelwall, delayed by morning traffic, towards the bus stop where I'd leap on to the open-backed vehicle, clutching my briefcase containing the tongue sandwiches and leaky orange juice bottle, choking in my blue school tie, only just catching the bus but joyful to have missed the train.

Two stops along the route, in Urmston, Malcolm Russell would board, with his shock of red hair and his broad grin – my five-year-long companion on the journey. Both of us pretended to fancy girls and both of us were absorbed in our religious beliefs, the latter filling many hours of discussion as he was a Jehovah's Witness and I was an evangelical and each of us felt conscience-bound to convert the other. I think, looking back, that the conversations were pretty sophisticated for thirteen-year-olds; both of us read our Bibles pretty thoroughly and were fired up to defend our versions of the Faith.

The girl issue – well, unlike the lunchboxes, it was never unpacked. I said I fancied one girl on the bus and he said he fancied another girl on the bus, but both of us were hiding in those days of hiding. I never fancied Malcolm, which was just as well. It would have made our daily bus ride a time of adolescent frustration and pain. Sex was very often on our lips though, and we'd talk about filthy things in a prurient manner: 'The *sins* people commit, oooh it's just disgusting, men lying with other men, forbidden by the Bible, an abomination! Pornography – it should be banned.' But then I'd tease Malcolm about nipples or pubic hair or a bulge in his trousers ('it's only linen') – our dizzy dance between fascination and fulmination. Malcolm had a way of saying certain words which dissected them as it stretched them. 'E . . . rec . . . tion' seemed to extend well beyond its three syllables as his eyes flashed with fun, fire and fear.

We were bright boys, with original ideas and a certain flair, but for some reason we failed to work at school. It was not laziness as such, just a kind of psychic inertia, an inability to step on to the steady conveyor belt of academic demands. We both did badly in our exams yet we both read voraciously and had opinions (thought through, if immature and weird) about many topics. At a better school, with more inspiring (or even competent) teachers, we might have flourished.

## Lennox Berkeley's umbrella

Nicholas Ashton, the pianist and teacher, became one of my closest friends only when I left Chetham's to go to the Royal Northern College aged fifteen. It's strange that we only began to correspond and spend time together then because we'd been at the same school for the previous five years. We were not in the same year but I was always keenly aware of him – his quick walk across the courtyard with darting glances to left and right, his eccentric absent-mindedness behind the thick glasses, his neatly folded black umbrella nearly always by his side, and, as often as not, a score of Lennox Berkeley about his person. We laugh about this still because that compositional obsession lasted only a short while, but I can see him now, along a corridor at Chets, with the Berkeley Preludes or Piano Concerto under the arm not carrying the umbrella.

But just as Berkeley is more French than English in his sensibilities, so Nicholas always seemed more continental than British to me. He had (has) a natural elegance, a way of savouring beautiful things which enhances their allure. A picnic with him would consist of, say, a wonderful hunk of cheese, and as he unwrapped it the Stilton's veins seemed as if painted by Chardin. He couldn't light a cigarette (and he lit many) without a sense of style, calling to mind glamorous movie stars from Hollywood's tobacco years. His tie seemed to hang with a nonchalance unexpected in Manchester's grime of the time; a croissant sourced, bought and impeccably served had an extra buoyant crispness. One of the most colourful people I've met, he was like a classic black and white photograph come to life – shot by Man Ray or Cecil Beaton perhaps.

Like Malcolm Russell, I never fancied him in a sexual way but I was in awe of him, and intimidated by his intelligence. He seemed to exude an air of intellectual confidence and exploration that was beyond me. He was Virginia Woolf to my Harold Robbins. His fawn raincoat flapped around his satchel on the school courtyard as if he were about to direct a movie about the French Resistance rather than attend a mediocre history lesson in a dilapidated classroom. Although he was a wonderful pianist and a penetrating musician (his glorious Schubert in particular), for me *he* was the art work. Like Oscar Wilde or Andy Warhol, his personality was the piece.

I was honoured when we became friends, but soon giggling and merriment replaced reverence. We wrote long, pretentious letters to each other about books we'd half read. We smoked cigarettes on the sofas of posh Manchester department stores, tipping the ash into overpriced ashtrays on glass side tables. We went in search of the perfect astrakhan coats despite lacking the money to buy them or the wardrobes of Tite Street to house them . . . and in spite of the incredulous looks of the tailors of Ancoats. 'What do you want it for?' asked Mr Rosenfield. 'To walk the streets,' I replied, not entirely unaware of the hidden meaning that those words might have. I fully realised the implications, though, as I put down the packet of Knorr's Cheddar-flavoured powder once at the cash register of the Co-op in Latchford, Nicholas at my side, saying, with a sibilant lisp: 'Jussst the cheessse sssauccce pleassse.'

We're still close friends forty-plus years later and there could be many episodes in this book beginning: do you remember that time when . . . we drove my mother's car onto the beach and got stuck in the sand? We had to release it by stuffing a volume of Beethoven sonatas under the back tyre. The car was filthy after we escaped, covered with wet sand. How on earth did we think that we could clean it and hide our escapade by vigorously rubbing the scum off? My mother was understandably furious at the forest of scratches all over its black bonnet.

## Knee up

I suppose it's called a nervous breakdown, although that seems too grand a term at this remove, too substantial, too definitive. But at the time it felt dreadful.

I must have been about eleven or twelve, in my second year at Chetham's, and I became obsessively afraid of being mugged. Then I *was* mugged. Leaving school one afternoon I turned the corner past the cathedral to the bus stop, and there were three lads by the shelter, lounging-leaning lads, lazy in the thick minutes between cigarettes and curses. 'You got some money?' one of them asked as I walked up in my blue school uniform, bare legs goose-bumped above the ridden-down socks. I didn't answer. Yes? No? What did it matter when aggression was in the air and the thing I most feared in the world was unfolding before me? 'You got any MONEY?' His voice was raised now and the other kids had come closer, three-in-one, a bristling malevolence. 'I don't have any money,' I said. The speaker slunk towards me and my stomach lurched as he punched my arm and then my stomach – light strokes, as I remember, but heavy with po-tential. I prepared for the worst but they just laughed and walked away. I began to cry, more from relief than from pain.

As I wiped my eyes an older businessman walked up to me. A smile of false teeth, a gleam of spittle on the lip. 'Are you alright, young man?' He moved in close, where the boys had huddled just before, and somehow I sensed a different kind of danger. I was relieved by his presence, which might protect me if the boys returned, but when he offered to take me to his office for a cup of tea I flinched inside. 'No thank you. I'm fine. My bus will be here soon.' And, as if my dis-tress were a signal, the number 3 arrived and I was safe again. On board. With the ticket collector. The worn leather seats. The bell ringing before each stop. My briefcase on my knees.

I just didn't want to go to school after that. I was terrified to leave the house. My father would drive me to Manchester when he could manage it, but as often as I could I would just stay at home and watch television, feeling left out of life, sad and not knowing why. The problem with any mental stress is that we need our mind to cure our mind, and that's precisely what's not functioning properly. We can't see psychological wounds, touch them, mess with them, dress them with ointment and a bandage. They fester behind a locked door.

My mother took me to the doctor and I tried to explain to him what I felt, that feeling of just being frightened. He asked my mother to leave the room for a few minutes and she went outside to the waiting area. He looked at me closely then looked away, all the time fiddling with his gold fountain pen, his cuffs thick and their gold links chunky. 'So you're scared of being mugged then?' He was smiling, it seemed with professional sympathy. 'Just stand up, will you?' I stood up from the chair and he stood up from the other side of his desk, walking around the side slowly towards me. 'You're afraid of them mugging you, aren't you?' His voice had risen and he was now standing close, right in front me. I could smell his breath. His body stiffened. 'You mean like this?' He drew his knee up sharply, quickly into my groin and I let out an anguished scream. My mother came rushing in. 'What the heck is going on?' she demanded, with an anger just short of losing the deference we feel we must show to those in authority. This, after all, was the man who prescribed her own depression medication. 'Oh don't worry, Mrs Hough,' he chortled, suddenly the friendly uncle as he retook his seat behind the desk in front of the leather blotter. 'I didn't touch him. It's all in his mind. I was faking it to see if he would react.'

Whether the pain was indeed in my imagination or whether his knee had slipped or whether he had really intended to hurt me . . . who knows? But his behaviour was seriously unethical at the least and I felt strangely violated and lonely afterwards. Twirling open the gold fountain pen, he wrote out a prescription for some tablets as well as a medical note which gave me permission to stay at home and watch all the television I wanted. I think I missed out most of that academic year one way or another and everything began a slow decline over the next three years to my wretched O levels, which I scraped through with mediocre grades. I lost interest in the piano after that too, barely practising as my hair grew longer and the rock records played louder.

I can see that doctor's room to this day. Next to the sweet shop on Barley Road.

## My purple bedroom and my wasted years

I had my bedroom ceiling painted deep purple and the walls a sort of creamy mauve. Posters were blu-tacked there which had been torn out of *Jackie* magazine (they kept a copy for me each week at the newsagent's): Donny Osmond, Marc Bolan, David Cassidy, shirts unbuttoned to the navel, smiles just for me. The songs were a cover for the crushes. The piles of LPs. Clive Lythgoe and *Keyboard Giants of the Past* were downstairs with the radiogram. I had the groovy stuff up in my purple room – Alice Cooper, T. Rex, and, later, Led Zeppelin and Emerson, Lake & Palmer as my rock began to prog.

With joss sticks burning I used to do yoga, naked, on the floor of this bedroom under the purple ceiling, the lotus to 'Black Dog', the plough to 'Dead Babies'. To stop anyone coming in when I had my legs in the air I would stuff two *Reader's Digest* magazines in the gap under the door. My bedroom was somewhere to hide. To hide my quickening heart in front of the half-naked posters. To hide the schoolbooks unread, yawning as the pages unturned. To hide my spotty face. Hideaway. The word suggests something cosy and fun. The reality was a cover for the ache of adolescence.

Then, with lights finally out, to hide inside the bed – although this was little comfort because for years my mother bought us nylon sheets. Perhaps the breathless bedding was some protection against the winter's freeze as there was no central heating in the house, but after the first warm minutes there followed eight restless hours of boil-in-the-bag oppression. Not to mention the snag of toenails, which made each movement of the leg an annoyance. And if a limb chose to move quickly, or had an involuntary jerk during a dream, there was an electric shock – sheets suddenly alive with a spark, fireflies darting inside pyjamas.

Of course, the piano was still downstairs but somehow I don't remember playing it much. It didn't delight me as it had. Practising was like another hour of homework, to get done as quickly as possible. And what homework did I have? I remember nothing, just television, hours and hours of it, up to six hours a night. And when I failed to go to school, even more. *Rainbow, Pebble Mill at One, General*

*Hospital, Crown Court, Jackanory, Blue Peter*, the six o'clock news, *Look North, Emmerdale Farm* (the 'farm' was later dropped from the title), *Crossroads, Bless This House, Love Thy Neighbour, Dad's Army, The Goodies, Porridge, World in Action, Panorama*, the nine o'clock news – in case anything had changed during three hours of watching telly. Solidly staring at the box. Safe in Cheshire, in the 1970s, by the fire. I think back and simply don't understand it.

*Coronation Street* was my mother's favourite programme and for a while the opening theme music was my signal to go to bed: 'Now, up the stairs. I'm going to count to three: one, two . . .' – all of this whilst the cat slunk across Weatherfield's terraced roofs in the opening credits, accompanied by the saxophone's smoky melody. Then I had a birthday (was it my ninth?) when one of my new privileges was that I could stay up on Mondays and Wednesdays and actually *watch Coronation Street*. But now the music at the end was my signal to go to bed. Horrid on the summer nights when the evening light blazed through my thin curtains.

## David Bowie

In the dining room, where I practised the piano as little as I could (a passage scrambled? Oh well, that'll do for today) there was a chipped bust of Beethoven which wobbled next to my underused metronome. But upstairs, stuck onto the purple bedroom walls, were those posters of my real heroes. And none was more prominently displayed than electric-shock-orange-haired David Bowie. And none more strange.

The weird-whine voice, the sparkling costume, the boyish physique, the girlish smile – a bizarre imaginary companion for a Cheshire schoolboy. The BBC's *Top of the Pops* was where I first heard him, hugging his blue guitar, sharing the microphone with another handsome singer, two male heads tense with music, arms around each other, shouting their song through each other's spittle. 'There's a Star—MAN waiting in the sky', the same octave leap as Judy Garland's 'Some—WHERE over the rainbow'. The top note in both songs was a voice- and heart-breaker. The world belonged to the young. The childish imagery of *The Wizard of Oz* might be okay for kids but for an immature thirteen-year-old like me it was passé and old-fashioned.

I didn't do drugs or sex, but rock 'n' roll was my life for a few years. My drug was the psychedelic world of stars like Bowie; sex was gazing at the open shirts and tight trousers of glam rock's provocation as the records turned and scratched and wore out on my hi-fi system. David Bowie filled my time as I wasted my time, staying home from school, my whole life a 1970s three-day week. But I'm not sure all was lost. The space that era created in many imaginations might have been akin to the moon landing a few years earlier. We were able to look down from the spaceship and see our planet from a different perspective. The (Jean) Genie was out of the bottle.

The politics of pop stars is often naive, but perhaps the

anarchy and wild imagination expressed in songs like Bowie's, as the planet itself was poised for destruction at the touch of a button, allowed for a release of tension in anxious youth. Weapons of mass destruction are rarely painted purple.

## Yes, I pulled down his trunks

After my traumatic experience being pushed in the deep end at Chetham's we decided it was time for me to learn to swim. So for a while I used to go along on Saturday mornings with my father to Warrington Baths, at the time an unrestored Victorian monstrosity. The changing rooms were little cabins all around the pool with swinging half-doors, the upper area only half-covered with flimsy, flapping, canvas curtains. It was all pretty much open to public view so women had their own separate changing area. I would be lying if I said that our trips to Warrington Baths were pleasurable only because of the time spent learning how to move in the water; the row of naked men towelling their chests dry alongside the pool had its own allure.

But the pleasure was not unmitigated. Because you walked directly from the street through puddles of water to get to each cabin, outdoor shoes trailing grime and constant splashes from the pool adding to the mix, the floor was a disgusting quagmire of mud and filth. Woe betide the one who dropped an item of clothing whilst getting dressed, or who was unable to balance on the top of a shoe whilst drying between the toes of the other foot. It was a foul environment

My paternal grandmother,
Hilda Smith.

I never met my paternal
grandfather, Thomas Victor
Iorwerth Hough. But then
neither did my father . . .

My parents, in a photo probably taken before I was born. My mother, outgoing
and extrovert; my father, shy and thoughtful. It was not a happy marriage.

Taken in the 1950s, in the early years of my parents' marriage. My father was always very chivalrous. 'Take care to walk on the outside when out with a lady, near to the kerb.'

A child is born and a cravat replaces the tie.

My mother holding me, flanked by her parents. Her sister, Eileen, is at the back, as if left out of the picture. My father has now lost the cravat.

A determined little boy.

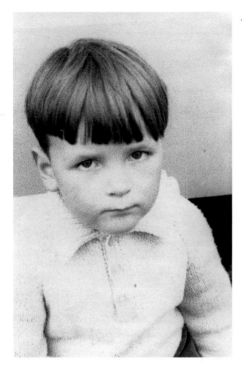

Probably at Criccieth, the year of the pink stilettos.
Liz Foster (Auntie Liz) treads water on the left.

In my grandparents' garden.

I was a terrible cellist. That's Jean Sheppard in the background.
I think it's her house.

Proud teacher: Heather Slade and me.

The Thelwall Rose Queen Festival. I won second prize as Liberace (note the candelabra), dressed in a suit made by my grandmother.

Mr Ellsworth     Mrs Stobbs

Winnie     Constance     Jean     Mavis
Monk       Bradburn    Sheppard   Delooze

The teachers at Thelwall County Primary in the late 1960s.

On the lawn at Dartington Summer School in 1978. Andrew Parrott, the conductor, has his back to us. On Andrew's right is Gordon Green, next to whom is my mother. It was during this week that I first attended a Catholic Mass, at Buckfast Abbey.

in which to go swimming and I caught more than one verruca there over the years.

Later there was Broomfields Leisure Centre in Appleton –
sometimes playing badminton with friends, and sometimes
swimming too. Once I'd learned to swim, my breaststroke
became quite vigorous: 'Reach out and then pull down, deep
strokes,' my teacher instructed me. All very well, except . . .
on one occasion, swimming from left to right, no glasses or
goggles or contact lenses, blurred or blind, reaching, pulling, deep, reaching, pulling, and I was almost at the rail.
One more reach, one more deep pull – but instead of the
rail, I inadvertently reached out for another man's swimming
trunks, fingers inside his waistband, then vigorously pulled
down. As I spluttered out of the water, gasping, horrified,
swallowing water, I saw an angry face. 'What the bloody hell
. . .' 'Oh, I'm so sorry,' I choked, desperately treading water.
'I . . .' Nothing I could say could explain or change the fact
that I had actually reached out in a public swimming pool
and pulled down a stranger's trunks.

Ah, and before I forget, I was responsible for another
person's trunks ending up below the hips at the same venue.
Nicholas Ashton, on one of his regular visits to stay at our
house, had suggested we go for a swim. So I lent him a
spare pair of trunks I had, in a hideous beige and brown
crinkly material with three plastic gold buttons down the
front. We drove out to Broomfields and changed. He was
more than slightly embarrassed at this ghastly swimming
costume so he hurried out of the changing room to dive

swiftly into the pool where it could be hidden under the water. As his body sliced through the surface the trunks flew off and ended up around his ankles. I stood at the side engulfed in laughter as he bent down with a furious fluster to pull them up. Strangely enough I was not banned from attending this sports centre after these two events; indeed, the delightful Angie, and her son, Graeme, who both worked there at the time, kept in touch with me until her death forty years later.

## Whatever you do, don't turn out queer

Words of my mother's sister, Eileen, echoing across my childhood. We'd visit her at Christmas, and after parking the car in her drive, we'd gather the presents together. If I happened to pick up my mother's handbag along with the mince pies she would rush out of the house in a panic: 'Put that handbag down, Stephen. You'll turn out queer.' Later on, comically, it was even a risk when *meeting* gay people. 'Oh Stephen, you might catch it' – like same-sex attraction could sneak upon one like the flu or measles. When she saw an email from my female manager many years later with 'love' and 'xxx' she thought it was from a girlfriend. She couldn't have been happier if she'd won the lottery. 'Oh no, Ei. Dominique wears leathers and rides a motorbike. She's a lesbian.' Her face collapsed with bitter disappointment until I started laughing and she knew it was a joke. A different kind of disappointment set in when I admitted that Dominique was *not* gay, and Eileen kept hoping, with increasing desperation over the years, that neither was I.

Being gay is one of my oldest memories, both conscious and subconscious. From the earliest years homosexuality was a pulse, not so much of desire but of identity. I recognised it in the music I played, in my sensibilities and interests, in my sense of humour . . . and in the attraction I felt for boys. 'Mummy, why does my willy grow bigger?' I cried out this question at a lull in a dinner party once to titters of amusement around the table. But I knew what I was saying. I meant it to be naughty and a little outrageous, and it wasn't really a question. It was an assertion of identity: a joke, a tease, an erotic spark. I was not yet ten years old.

Homophobia is a strange word when it means objection to, or dislike of, homosexuals (itself a strange word). Not everyone who hates something is fearful of it. But where homophobia really kicks in is when the fear is inside myself, when I sense there is something rooted in me which causes me to be afraid. When every street seems straight, but mine twists. I'm Broadway amongst so many vertical Avenues. Homophobia? Yes, fear of parents' rejection, then friends', then society's, then the Church's, then God's. Sex itself is complex enough, when out of childhood's innocent grass the first snake appears; but puberty's routine gaucheries for the straight boy are a hand cut off for the gay boy. The beginnings of sexual interest for the straight boy mean that the family is safe, at least for another generation; for the gay boy it's 'Leave this house. You are no longer my son.' A new family has to be found: head to the metropolis, only prison to be avoided.

I never felt such an extreme reaction to homosexuality from my parents but there were snarky remarks along the way, whether about Larry Grayson mincing across our television screen or a famous pop star's gay/Christian conflict. At one point I decided to try to show more physical affection towards my father, a hug perhaps (goodness knows why the sudden change), and I remember my mother saying, 'Colin, don't let him do that. He'll turn out queer.' I made a mental note and, again, quietly closed the closet door. But then, fast forward forty years, when my mother was living her final years in the nursing home: 'Dennis is like my second son,' she proudly told the cook. 'My son's gay and he's got a lovely partner. He's an *ornamental*.' From Taiwan, although there was some confusion as to whether that was Thailand. It all meant the same for one whose furthest fling was her honeymoon on the Isle of Man.

But in New York in the early years of AIDS I was more afraid that if I happened to get sick, people back home would know I was gay than that I would die prematurely in my twenties. I remember thinking at least once, when flying across the Atlantic, that if we crashed into the ocean I would at least avoid having to reveal my sexual identity. I even enquired about doing some charity work at an AIDS hospice so that, if I became infected, I might have an excuse: 'Yes, I cut my finger once as I was tending to Alvin. That must have been it.' I could be Father Damien amongst his lepers – a saint, not a slut.

'Whatever you do, don't turn out queer.' Homophobia? What's not to fear?

## My mother's lady friends

My memories of my mother are intertwined with memories of her friends, a procession of women throughout her life, usually unmarried, companions and sometimes (in the mildest form) servants.

I've mentioned Auntie Liz, the nurse who lived near to us in my earliest years and who actually delivered me into this world. Later on she moved to a charming thatched cottage in Burton with warped beams and sloping ceilings and we'd visit often. My mother told me Liz was in love with my father. I didn't doubt it. I adored Liz and she is central to so many memories of my childhood, including many family holidays when she would join us. She had a flesh-coloured tag mole on her neck which she insisted was made larger by my playing with it incessantly as a toddler. She had a large cleavage into which things would drop from time to time. I remember the crumbs from a Cadbury Curly Wurly and, alarmingly on one occasion, a burning cigarette.

Later there was Marguerite, posh-voiced Marguerite, who spent her professional life teaching in tiny private schools in Cheshire – Victorian houses turned into expensive classrooms. I never held my knife incorrectly ('Gilbert Harding said, "I can't *abide* people who hold their knives like pencils,"' she exclaimed once), but I did used to say 'pleased to meet you' as a greeting. '"How do you do" is the correct form, Stephen.' I've not forgotten. I've met hundreds of people with a handshake and Marguerite's phrase since then. She was unmarried like most of my mother's friends and lived in an upstairs flat on Whitbarrow Road, Lymm, with an elderly, also unmarried, aunt. Splendid rice puddings would emerge from her Aga when we visited – leathery burnt-cream tops with thick-textured rice. I don't know if my mother and Marguerite ever shared a bed but they certainly seemed to spend a lot of time cuddling. 'You're like two lesbians' said my aunt Eileen to her once, with a snort of disgust.

Marguerite had bad eyesight and couldn't read easily so I offered to help her out. She was delighted but then, as I was going through my intense Catholic conversion period at the time, I would bring along propaganda writings about the One True Church: *The Faith of Millions* by Father O'Brien was a favourite (of mine, I doubt hers) with its charts proving that Luther was wrong and Rome was right. This deeply committed Anglican bore with me cheerfully and, as I think back, with an heroic charity.

There was Cynthia too, married but obsessed with my mother. They prayed together and 'spoke in tongues' in Bible studies. Cynthia would ring the doorbell on occasion and hand over a cake, and she always seemed overawed and nervous with my mother. Then there was Hilda, who for a while came to our house often and then . . . she no longer came to our house. I really liked Hilda and said regularly to my mother, 'Why don't you phone Hilda? . . . You should get in touch with Hilda . . . Let's go and visit Hilda.' 'Oh, I will' . . . but she didn't. Even the Christmas cards ceased. And there were more. Gertrude: 'I loved sex, couldn't get enough,' this twice-widowed septuagenarian once told me, in her lilting Welsh accent. And unmarried Winifred, a jolly, gentle soul who, like Marguerite, had spent her life teaching in small private schools (in Canada and New Zealand), but unlike Marguerite had no posh accent to show for it.

## Jimmy Savile – twice

A short time after his death Jimmy Savile went from being the BBC's secular saint to being the very symbol of depravity. 'He is a homosexual, isn't he?' commented Gordon Green's wife, Dorothy, in the mid-1970s. I thought it a strange re-mark at the time when, on his television shows, he always seemed to have a young woman bouncing on his knee. Was it prompted by his flamboyance? Or maybe it was the thick cigar, a burning fiery phallus grasped between his knuckle-buster ringed fingers? Or maybe Mrs Green saw something malevolent behind the screen and gay was her reflex, her go-to response for something sexually distasteful.

For some reason, whilst I was at Chets, I was invited to be on two of his shows. *Clunk Click* was the first (its name came from the seatbelt campaign advert on the telly: 'Clunk Click Every Trip') and there I was, in 1970-something, in my school's Tudor uniform, a cassock with bright yellow socks, playing the Paganini/Liszt Etude *La Chasse*. 'Why have you chosen this particular piece, Steve?' asked the Liszt-lookalike (both sported long, whitish hair and had large, protruding moles). 'Because you're always chasing about, Mr Savile.' Neither foxes nor skirts were on my innocent mind – but it did get a laugh from the studio audience.

I also played a piece I'd written called *Walkabout*. Dedicated to him. A kind of gigue in A minor. I was an ambitious enough composer then to hope that he might really like it and might even use it as the theme music for his programme. He didn't, but a year or two later my school received a call from the producer of *Jim'll Fix It*, Savile's later, better, better-known show in which youngsters wrote in to get Jim to fix up a dream they had – hang-gliding, or riding a camel, or any number of things. Jimmy wanted a student from Chets to come on the show and play duets with John Lill, and I was the one chosen. It was awkward from the start because I had to pretend that I'd written in to request this 'fix', and, as far as I knew, John Lill was unaware of the story behind his being asked to fulfil my dream. 'What is it about my playing that you like so much?' asked John over lunch with me and my dad. A reasonable question in the circumstances. 'It's your interpretation, Mr Lill,' replied the gauche northern boy with the flared trousers and the patches of pimples. We played the *Jamaican Rumba* by Arthur Benjamin on the show, and then Jimmy bounded over to the piano, beaming, wagging his cigar. 'So what do you think of our boy Steve, then?' 'He shows much promise,' replied John. And as if to prove it Jimmy put a new score on the music rack.

'OK, so let's see how you both do sight-reading this.' The fixing continued because this worn-out copy of 'Le Bal' by Bizet, now slightly smelling of a Havana cigar, was actually my own score, brought down with me on the train to Euston that morning, the pencil markings of Heather Slade hastily erased ('steady rhythm, don't rush, don't force the tone'). We romped through 'Le Bal' and that was it. I think it was on that same day that I met Gary Glitter backstage, whom Jim had fixed for someone else. Or was that on the *Clunk Click* set in March 1974 when the pop star had famously appeared before the cameras before disappearing into Savile's dressing room? I got his autograph ('it's not for me'). All is a dream for me now; for others it was their worst nightmare.

## Bell bottoms

I can't remember the first time clothes meant more to me than merely covering my body. I suppose it was in the early 1970s when I was scouring *Jackie* magazine for posters to tack on my bedroom wall and then watching those stars appearing on *Top of the Pops* in their bell bottoms and platform shoes. I had examples of both – a pair of jeans which were entirely patches, the denim itself stitched into squares. No more hideous garment ever spread over legs, and spread was the word. The flares were voluminous tents covering my shoes in a giant flap of trailing, fraying fabric. Shoes best covered. My tottering pair were in purple and green. I waddled around in them with a fuzzy, unshaven face and my breaking voice. I thought I was ready for the catwalk in that outfit. Also I wore medallion-type things. I had a huge key (Tower of London huge) on a yellow shoelace around my neck. It was red and black and bumped against my chest as I walked or played the piano – 'neither use nor ornament' as the saying goes.

Cheesecloth shirts. I loved my pink one with its pattern of blue and white birds: 'When I get chest hairs they will poke through.' Oh really? Where? On the beach at Torremolinos? Then there was the identity bracelet. It had not been engraved but I wanted STEVE to appear on the silver band. Weird, as I've never really been a Steve. Only Jimmy Savile and my parents called me that. For one month perhaps I thought it would make me cool. After all, nothing else in those years did. It is tarnishing in a drawer somewhere, without the engraving. I wonder if it still smells of the Hai Karate aftershave I used to shake onto my wrists?

And then the memories fade, but I imagine a landfill somewhere in Cheshire still contains some of my never-rotting 1970s dreck . . . immortal birds, eternal flares.

## Not the Knot Garden!

As I've suggested earlier, I listened to very little classical music in my early teens; but Heather once left a copy of Michael Tippett's Second Piano Sonata at our house and I decided to learn it. I was fascinated with this astringent work, my first taste of non-tonal musical language, and I loved the bemused reaction it received from my parents as I practised it at home – like biting on a lemon. I mentioned it to Gordon Green. 'I'm not sure I can help you much with a piece like that. It's not quite my style. Still, bring it along.' To guide me I bought a recording by John Ogdon and on the other side of the LP was an even greater revelation: Tippett's ecstatic Piano Concerto, a lyrical outpouring originally inspired by hearing Walter Gieseking play Beethoven's Fourth Concerto. The opening of the Tippett Concerto instantly cast a spell over me which remains to this day. The vast space created in the orchestra from the deep string C under the soil of the earth to the tinkle of piano arpeggios tracing a delicate tune above the treetops was completely mesmerising.

The Second Sonata is from Tippett's second period, which includes his opera *King Priam*. By the early 1960s he had left behind the earlier verdant lushness of the Piano Concerto and the musically related opera *The Midsummer Marriage*, with all their succulent fruits of the forest. His language sharpened and he began to write music of granite-edged severity, with non-melodic motifs and angular textures: from lemonade to lemons.

So I was listening to Tippett when I was listening to little else – and I soon moved on to his third opera, *The Knot Garden*, even buying a vocal score of it with my pocket money. Tippett visited Manchester on one occasion when I was at Chets and gave a talk at the Royal Exchange Theatre which I attended. I remember his sandals. Afterwards I queued up to get his autograph, clutching the fat, bright green score of the opera. I finally arrived in front of his seat and handed it to him and he started slightly, looked up at the teenager standing there, and smiled with a sparkle in his eye. He didn't say anything but I remember that encounter clearly. For one second there was a discharge of energy: God and Adam's fingers almost touched.

## Cello, drums and flute

It was suggested at some point (maybe by Heather) that I should have a second instrument, and for some reason I chose the cello. We bought one from somewhere and I began lessons with Sister André at Seafield Convent of the Sacred Heart of Mary in Crosby, near Liverpool. It was a grammar school for girls and my mother would drive me there on Saturdays for my lessons. Sister André, dressed in those times in full religious garb, was brisk, fresh-faced, kind and, for me, extremely exotic. Later I went to study with Lesley Shrigley Jones at her home in one of Altrincham's larger Victorian houses, and then, once I was at Chetham's, I was assigned to Robert Howarth for my lessons. I really loved the sound of the cello but hated everything else to do with it – carrying it on the bus, hauling it up the stairs of Palatine House, tuning it, putting rosin on the bow, and then . . . the sounds I made as I scratched out my W. H. Squire pieces. I passed ABRSM Grade 5 (with a lowish mark) and gave up, switching to percussion. I can't really play anything on the cello now, although Steven Isserlis has commented on my 'remarkable' vibrato.

In contrast I relished my percussion studies with Max and Irene Molin, a married couple both of whom were in the Hallé Orchestra. I spent hours practising side-drum riffs on my rubber pad, and my parents even bought me a vibraphone which I ended up playing with Oscar Peterson's trio on the telly . . . a moment of acute embarrassment about which I will say no more. I've written about orchestral concerts at school in which I took part, playing alongside fellow students all of whom went on to brilliant musical careers, from Neil Percy, now percussionist in the London Symphony, to Wayne Marshall and Mike Lindup. For a brief time I learned the flute too. Janet Milone was my fantastic teacher, until the school said that I couldn't study three instruments so I'd have to choose between flute and percussion. As it was unlikely I'd get to play *Daphnis et Chloé* in the school orchestra I decided to stick with the drums. I can still get a note out of the flute, though, and did so on two of Sir James Galway's mighty, weighty instruments many years later. The rose-gold one was very elegant but the platinum one had the warmer tone, I felt . . .

## Henry Miller, my favourite writer

Warrington Public Library – we went there on Saturday mornings after going to the swimming baths next door. My father borrowed countless books every week but I tended just to browse around. Musical scores were to the left of the entrance and the only volume that sticks in my mind today is a large cream-coloured album of Malcolm Williamson's piano music. I can smell it today. I know why: Clive Lythgoe and that first LP. I wanted to learn every piece on that mixed recital. Williamson's 'Flower-Sellers'. A lilting tune by this Australian, almost but not quite an earworm, in 3/4 in G major, a *Gymnopédie* of sorts: Satie in the Outback.

The library had a card index housed in large cabinets of light wood drawers, and certain books had a special listing. I think they were stamped 'S' for special permission. I can't remember how I got to hear about the writers on that list but those were the ones I wanted to check out, anything that had been banned or deemed obscene: Henry Miller (*Tropic of Cancer, Tropic of Capricorn*); James Joyce (only *Ulysses*: *Finnegans Wake* was probably too complex to corrupt); Hubert Selby Jr (*Last Exit to Brooklyn* – I still haven't taken it); William Burroughs (*The Naked Lunch*); and, still in the 1970s, D. H. Lawrence (*Lady Chatterley* not *Kangaroo*). 'Do you know what your son is reading, sir?' piped the indignant lady librarian in a tweed skirt with half-moon spectacles. 'Oh, he's fine,' said my father, looking at me with a mischievous twinkle in his eyes.

Did I actually read those forbidden books? I think I just liked the whiff of scandal I caused when asking someone to go into the back to fetch them for me. I can see clearly the trajectory from the boy under the bed of Birch Road to the card index of Warrington Library. I was a shy kid, towel clasped against my nakedness at Warrington Baths, Bible in the purple bedroom; but then I was unblushing and fascinated from my earliest years by sex: those pop-star posters on that purple bedroom's walls. The prurient Puritan. 'He's got bedroom eyes,' said one of my mother's unmarried friends a few years later. Why only in the bedroom?

## Dover Road

Marshall Cherry could have stepped straight out of the pages of J. B. Priestley's *The Good Companions*. I remember always a three-piece suit and a soft pink face, all innocent smiles, but with iron-clad, clear convictions underneath. I remember too that he added aitches to some words and left aitches off other words: Hadam and Heve in the garden of Heden.

Mr Cherry was the senior elder of Gospel Hall, an evangelical church in Latchford that shirked denominational monikers but was basically Plymouth Brethren. There were three such churches in Warrington within a three-mile radius: Forster Street (the most strict), Bethesda (more lax) and us at Dover Road (somewhere in the middle). Lax meant that not all the ladies wore head coverings (St Paul did demand it after all); strict meant that one wondered if the ladies ever actually removed their hats.

But not only did women have to wear hats, they were not permitted to speak in the church. And when I was given a lift from our home in Thelwall (a two-mile drive) with the Delooze family I had to sit in the front of the car, with the ladies squashed in the back, despite my being a mere teenager. A last gasp of Victorian values – Mr Cherry would probably have been seventy in 1970 so his parents would have celebrated more than one jubilee of the great queen.

Mrs Delooze taught me at Thelwall County Primary and she played the little electric organ at Dover Road, singing along with a tremolo worthy of a Wurlitzer, so that must have been the link to my going there in the first place. I soon became convinced that their literal reading of the Bible was correct and that within the plain blue walls of the meeting house (decorated with just one verse of Scripture stencilled in red and gold, close to the ceiling above the plain pulpit) there could be found an integrity hard to find elsewhere. After my vague, grey Anglican life at All Saints Church the bright, rock-solid certainties of Dover Road were dazzling.

For young people doubt is not generally regarded as something to be embraced: convictions should be concrete; to vacillate is to be cowardly and weak. One of the joys of getting older is to be able to recognise the wisdom of an uncertain mind, but for me, aged about thirteen, the Brethren's absolutism seemed unassailable. The Bible is wholly and entirely without error in every word – 'Amen', said I. And these people knew their Scripture. Always the King James Version, always in the finest tooled leather. Leather Bibles are a thing of beauty: the smell as they are prised out of the cardboard cover, the drape of the silk ribbon, the sewn signatures' blazing colour crust on the top and bottom of the spine, the indelible print. And the words themselves – the ringing melodic phrases which, with Shakespeare, are a foundation of the English language. There were no statues or stained-glass windows at Dover Road but these supple tomes cradled on tailored laps seemed to be a sort of sacrament, symbolising the docility of the soul in this rarefied world of regularity and commitment.

I got to know the look of the Bibles of my fellow worshippers. I remember when lovely, old, gentle Mr Reynolds bought a new one because his old one had literally worn out. The gold edges of the replacement's pages shone with the brilliance of the sun, and its scarlet leather in contrast to the retired black one seemed worthy of being enclosed in a case in a museum, so rich was its texture, so intense its colour, so warm its smell. As he opened it up to the Psalms or Colossians the thin pages were like the whisper of a silk fan. For these people their (tangible) Bibles were the closest companions of their lives.

I bought a big, new floppy one myself and a copy of the hymn book they used: *Sacred Songs and Solos*, an astonishing relic of another era. This collection was first published in the 1870s and was the fruit and tool of Moody and Sankey's missionary partnership. 'O wandering souls, why will you roam?'; 'Call them in – the poor, the wretched'; 'Still, still with Thee, when purple morning breaketh' – the words of the latter hymn were by Harriet Beecher Stowe, no less. Of course they were dated and quaint but even now I can sense the passion behind their sentiment, and the goodness of heart too. These were songs aimed to convert, yes, but also to console in times and situations of hopelessness for those spat out by the Industrial Revolution's assembly lines.

Many new varieties of Christianity flourished in the latter half of the nineteenth century, usually aiming to return to a more primitive practice of the faith along with a millennial, apocalyptic view of the world's future. Such were the changes in human life, in both society and science, that this fundamentalism was a comfort to those scared of change, sometimes a justified suspicion of passing fashion, fads and exploitation. It's understandable to want to preach about the End of the World when your own world is collapsing around you; it's tempting to call upon the judgement of God when justice appears lacking elsewhere.

My (two? three?) years at Dover Road were pretty intense. On Sundays three courses of evangelical devotion. After I had been baptised, full immersion of course, there was the morning Breaking of Bread service when only 'believers' could attend and take part, and where we sat silently in a circle (a square actually) with extempore prayer and Bible reading, as the Spirit led us. We even had a separate volume for singing in this service, *The Believer's Hymn Book* – and no organ accompaniment was allowed. I bought a copy of this book too, and 'believer' seemed to me a synonym for 'chosen'. If the Rapture should happen one Sunday morning, that tiny chapel in Latchford would be empty.

Like the Quakers, we sat in silence until someone felt moved to stand up and say something. The service always lasted about an hour (the Spirit was mindful of burnt Sunday roasts) and then Mr Cherry would go to get the loaf of bread and the decanter of non-alcoholic wine, the former unleavened and baked the night before by Mrs Cherry. It was more like an enormous scone and was passed around on a kind of silver platter, and we would pinch a knob from the rugged, rock-like surface. With strawberry jam and clotted cream it would have been quite delicious.

Then, after lunch back at home, back to the chapel for Bible study/Sunday school in the mid-afternoon; and then, at 6.30 in the evening, the Gospel Meeting. This was the service when it was hoped that those who were not already saved (accepting Jesus Christ as their personal saviour) would be touched and transformed. It's where I myself went forward aged about twelve or thirteen after a powerful sermon, with Mrs Delooze pulling out all the stops on the organ. Once I was 'saved' nothing could snatch that away; in this they differed from the Catholics, for whom salvation could theoretically go up in smoke with one lustful glance in which deliberate pleasure was taken. At Dover Road, once you were converted, Paradise was guaranteed . . . a powerful incentive to a restless youth.

It is easy to make fun of these meetings and the people whose lives were dominated by them. 'I begin reading my Bible and when I reach the end I start all over again. I find it refreshing.' Nothing more in life than to save souls and prepare for death; night and day's rotation as the flip and flop of a worn leather Bible's golden-edged pages. I lost interest after a while and began to attend less frequently. The world inside those doors, as safe as it might have seemed, was small. I became a 'backslider' and then, a number of years later, curious after the passing of time, I went back with a couple of friends to the evening Gospel Meeting, where I'd begun my journey. It seemed dotty, even comic. The hats, the three-piece suits, the sermon's ranting certainties. I wonder if the Gospel Hall is still there today, if the hymns are the same, if the blue chairs are in their old rows, if the walls have been repainted. 'Where is my wandering boy tonight?' asked the Victorian song. Still wandering. Aren't we all?

## Bibles and badges

The Bible Bookshop, a small establishment by Warrington's Bridge Foot (a poetic name for an ugly, traffic-jammed bottleneck) was a place to buy Christian books. I don't know quite why I had become obsessed with religion. I do remember the strained atmosphere in our house from my mother's charismatic prayer meetings but this wasn't my own path to faith. I'd been baptised a Methodist as a baby, confirmed an Anglican at junior school, but none of this meant very much to me. I hated praying before bedtime as a child and I worked out if I said 'Lord, help everyone' it would cover all bases, including mine.

But once I started attending Dover Road we would often visit the Bible Bookshop to browse. I remember picking up a book called *From Witchcraft to Christ* which literally scared me into belief at a time when my mind was at its most malleable and confused and fragile. I developed a terror of drugs and prostitutes and the destroyed lives which would result as

I read Doreen Irvine's memoir. I got to the point when I was petrified that someone might inject me with heroin as they walked past on the street, and that I'd become a hopeless addict, homeless, arms black with collapsed veins. This was followed by other similar sin-to-salvation books, such as *Run Baby Run* by Nicky Cruz, a powerful testimony about Puerto Rican street gangs in New York and the writer's conversion from violence and drugs to Christ. Now I can see that the authors of these books were overcome by the experience of God's unconditional love after lives scarred by violence and self-hatred. But strangely my connection to the stories was fear. I don't know how I got it all so wrong.

Apart from Bibles and other religious books I remember buying a lapel pin there, in blue, which I inserted into my school blazer: JESUS LIVES, it proclaimed. I had a lot of (gentle) mockery as I walked around the playground and corridors of Chetham's wearing this symbol of my faith, or the faith I wished I'd had. ('Wanting to believe is to believe,' said one archbishop. Most of us fail even to desire that desire.) A Catholic's crucifix, whilst more tangible, is also more diffuse. It is an identity badge and cultural marker, as well as a possible statement of faith. It both says more and less. In the same trinket box at the shop was an alternative badge: JESUS SAVES. In red, as I recall. I chose my slogan as one easier to defend and explain. Jesus saves . . . from what? Jesus lives? Well, it could be understood in various ways. It deflected the derision a bit.

Years later, after my conversion to Catholicism, I placed

a sticker in the rear window of my car: PRO PAPA. What good did that do? Well, it made me drive proudly to daily Mass. To the few who understood what it meant it was redundant. To others? It was (meant to be) a bullish marker, a red rag with its yellow and white papal flag on the side. It proclaimed that humans want to proclaim. To belong. To convert 'me against you' into 'us against them'. Flags, badges . . . wars.

## Bloody hell

The charismatic movement and a certain kind of feverish, weepy religious emotionalism is an unpleasant memory of my youth. Women came to our house to pray, in English and in the unintelligible outpourings of the Holy Spirit's Pentecostal tongues. Ladies who lurch – swaying and mumbling and crying out loud: 'Praise the Lord'; 'I hold her up to your healing love, O Jesus'; 'Hallelujah, praised be God'; 'If the Lord wills'. It really felt like the radiators had been pushed to their highest setting and the windows sealed shut. As these women hugged each other and wept on each other's shoulders one knew not the difference between the sickness and the cure.

The 'foreign tongues' at Pentecost, spoken of in the Acts of the Apostles, which led Americans in the nineteenth century to discover (invent?) Pentecostalism, were surely more Berlitz than Bedlam in the first century – the ability amongst a crowd of people from foreign lands to understand in their own languages something new and revolutionary, not some sort of spiritual cocaine. One of the beneficial aspects of organised religion is its inherent mediocrity. Excitable, impressionable humanity is forced inside an impersonal frame, tamed by routine, with built-in time for fads to run out of steam. Of course there is a need for passion and heroism, but always with a healthy suspicion of the constant shadow of vanity. It's hard to get the balance right.

My mother had had her initial religious conversion via the Church of England's evangelical wing. She had been to a revival meeting and thrown her pack of cigarettes into the aisle along with the heroin needles of others who were there: 'Come on, you older people! Cast away that tobacco. It's still a drug just the same,' shouted the visiting preacher. I'm certain that my mother's involvement in all this was a factor in the breakdown of both her nerves and her marriage. My father was not a Christian and the hothouse religiosity with its potential for smug moral judgements only pushed him further away. It was a phase for my mother, and it would be hard to reconcile the woman she later became with the woman she was then – or, indeed, the woman she had been before I was born. I remember her during this crisis, in bed with curtains drawn, women from the prayer group hovering around, praying, reading psalms, genuinely concerned. She was at peace, then a relapse, then at peace – an emotional seesaw with tears (and pills) accompanying both states.

In the midst of one of my mother's bad patches she became obsessed with Barbara Dickson and her hit song at the time. She would dance round the room seductively, wearing an orange kaftan. 'Answer me, oh my love; just what sin have I been guilty of?' crooned Barbara, and my mother's crush (it seemed like that to me at the time) was unbearably suffocating. My father would go upstairs, back to his Open University studies, or to memorise more Masonic ritual. Mum's hands above her head as the record turned one more time: 'Just what sin have I been guilty of?'

There was another occasion when we were driving with one of the leaders of the prayer group. She and my mother were in the front and I was on the back seat. The conversation was continually peppered with 'hallelujahs' and 'praise the Lords'. 'Mummy, you're not like this at home when you're saying bloody hell,' I piped from the rear. My mother had a 'look' for me when I was misbehaving. I think even today it would strike fear into my soul. She turned around in the car and gave me a choice example of it, teeth sucked in, lips tightened, brow furrowed, the laser-burning glare. If her religion had been genuine and life-enhancing she might have laughed at that point and said, 'Bloody hell, Steve, you're right!'

## My gregarious mother

Just as in fiction the most interesting characters are usually the villains, so in real life it can be much easier to talk about someone's negative qualities than their good ones. How do I get across my mother's warm heart and her sheer sense of fun which everyone who met her was enveloped by? The

ease with which people, even strangers, were able to open
their hearts to her. Every time we stopped to get petrol in
my childhood, before driving off it seemed that my mother
had made another lifelong friend with the attendant. Every
shop we went into she charmed the salesperson – whether
buying a sofa or a soda. Every plumber who came to plug
a leak, every electrician who came to fit a plug, in every
encounter she would create a situation of zest and friendship. She made people laugh, not so much with jokes but
with a carefree eccentricity which relished social interaction
and which seemed completely accepting and open. And
without a trace of sexual innuendo. She never flirted . . .
until the latter years when, in her eighties, she flirted so
shamelessly and so heavy-handedly that it made one gasp.
I'm convinced her gregarious nature would have made her a
success on stage. Indeed, I think she might have given Judy
Garland or Bette Midler a run for their money. A family
friend, Paul Cooper, crowned her a 'gay icon' and she accepted the title with pride.

I write in this book about her nervous breakdown and
about the difficulties she had with my father (the bottles
of Scotch before marriage and the bottles of valium afterwards), but this is only half the story. How can I convey
her goodness? The incredible dedication she had to me and
her supportive love over the years. I've seen many parents
in action, especially parents of young pianists, and I realise
how amazing my own were. How they gave me such encouragement whilst never forcing me into doing anything,

and having no eye for their own gain. They never saw my career as a way for themselves to become fulfilled or famous. And yet to tell this story requires clouds. Not only was there not a blue sky every day, but without clouds there would be no story. Clouds define the sky behind them. My parents' love for me was the changeless sky as I grew up, despite their foibles and their dysfunctional relationship.

There have been a number of times in my life when a telephone call to my mother changed everything. When I was uncertain about switching teachers at Juilliard, when I wasn't sure whether I should risk signing a lease on an apartment, and earlier, in moments of panic and distress at school, I would go to the corridor at Chets where there was a payphone and receive instant comfort when the pips had been silenced by the drop of a coin. There came a time much later when the roles were reversed, as she became more and more confused by her loss of memory. I always knew how to cheer her up, to calm her down. When I was a child I would call down in distress from my bedroom: 'Mummy, what can I think about?' Forty years later, leaving my Sydney hotel for the Opera House, I might get a tearful call of panic about something, but within a few minutes I'd get her laughing again. I think I learned the technique from her.

## The late Mr Hough

I'm not writing my parents' biography. Indeed, I'm not really even writing my own, but I suddenly feel a certain responsibility in writing about two people whom no one now knows and who were such strong personalities. I'm leaving so much out about my father – some of it by choice, some I never knew, some of it (his birth in Australia, his infancy in India) he didn't even know himself in any detail. I found one page in his papers with the following intriguing paragraph:

The details of my parents' meeting, subsequent second emigration from India to Australia, and the circumstances of their parting after my birth and early childhood are all subjects too complex to be dealt with adequately here – the full story up to my son Stephen's birth is distinctly off-beat and it is doubtful whether any popular women's magazine would accept it even as fiction. Perhaps it may be told at a later time.

He never told it to me. All I know is that my grandparents married in India, at St George's Anglican Church in Jamshedpur in 1926. Ship to Australia and grandfather's work in the steel industry in Mayfield, NSW. Grandmother left with Colin soon after his birth and boarded a ship back to India. 'Your father died' was the story she told him as they moved back to the United Kingdom. A lie. My grandfather, Thomas Victor Iorwerth (this last name indicating the family's Welsh connections over centuries), lived a further thirty-five Antipodean years, through another war, through another life, and actually died in 1961, the year I was born. As did his wife. The notice of my own parents' wedding

(6 September 1952) in the Prestatyn newspaper mentions my father's parents as 'Mrs Hilda Hough, The Highlands, The Brae, Meliden' and 'the late Mr T. Hough'. Late? He didn't even know it was happening.

## Red roses

I never remember any physical violence between my parents, but neither do I remember one moment of affection or tenderness, physical or verbal. Their marriage was a wedding cake without the cake: hard, brittle and cold. I arrived almost a decade after they married, their only child, weeks late out of the womb, pulled into the world with forceps, ill and bad-tempered. 'Your mother never wanted children,' my father told me, but I never felt unwanted or unloved for a second. I was the object of love for two people who didn't love each other. 'I married your father because my parents didn't like him': my mother's extraordinary, surely false admission in the bitter, later years of their marriage. On the contrary, their courtship appeared to have been a romantic one ('your father used to bring me a red rose every day'), and every now and then, I would see in her eyes a flash of admiration for him. Long after his death (she sat patiently by his bedside at the hospital) she said to me: 'Oh I forgave your father. He couldn't help it. He was oversexed . . . he had every woman in the village.' 'He looks a little gay in this army photo, Mum,' I said to her on another occasion, having dug out some old snapshots, one of which showed my father casting a limp arm around another soldier. 'Oh yes, he had men too, I imagine.'

Despite my father's love of sex he was highly chivalrous, even prudish, especially with women. I've mentioned that I never saw him naked, but I also remember that he told me never to swear or tell an off-colour joke in front of a lady. Always stand up when one entered the room; always try to walk on the outside of the path, nearest to the road, 'then if a car races through a puddle, you, not the lady, will get the worst of it'. Open the door for a woman, let her go first . . . and so on. All rather quaint in a twenty-first-century world of equality, but I think it illustrates that he was no forty-fifth President of the United States. He was naturally shy with women but never tongue-tied. He was reticent but with a sparkle. I see it now as a sort of technique of seduction – and it seems it worked. To this day, forty years after his death, people still say to me, 'Oh your father was so . . . charismatic/charming/colourful.'

He was always in good shape and, indeed, a bit of a fitness fanatic. In his youth he had boxed and played field sports. He founded the Health and Strength movement in Prestatyn after the war and later bought books on aerobics, going on punishingly long walks on the Pennine Way or Offa's Dyke. He always had the latest equipment: tents and boots and socks and thermal undergarments and thermos flasks. He had enough kit to join an Arctic trek – and even mentioned wanting to do that. 'Can you pay the bills first, Colin?' I still have one of the inner jackets he bought at that time. In the winter chills of Minnesota one year it passed the test.

I spoke to my mother's sister, not long before she died: 'Eileen, if you can remember anything about my parents when I was a kid just jot it down on a bit of paper.' 'Well, I caught your dad once snogging one of your teachers in the back of the car. I had to take you off for an ice cream. Oh, and he was always taking you to Jane Hitchens's house. "I don't like going to Auntie Jane's because they leave me in the kitchen to play and daddy goes off upstairs with Auntie Jane," you'd say.' Oh dear, those weren't quite the memories I had in mind, Eileen. Decades later, after I'd played a concert with the Liverpool Philharmonic Orchestra, this same Auntie Jane came backstage to see me. I barely remembered her and certainly didn't recognise her. She introduced herself and told me how fond she had been of my father. He was long dead at this point. 'I still think of him often, and I've kept a vase which has special memories for me. You see, he used to bring me a red rose every time he came to visit.'

## Eileen, anything more to add?

Well I just hope I'm not going to be in it that's all I can say what on earth do you want to write your memoirs for you don't want to tell everyone your secrets people will get the wrong end of the stick well as long as I'm not in it you can do what you want but don't say I didn't warn you. Do I have any memories? Well I suppose I do cos your mum and me were

sisters after all and I met your dad when your mum met him
at the Methodist Youth Club in Prestatyn anyway you know
that your dad was born in Australia in Mayfield. He didn't
remember anything about it but there seems to have been a
bit of bother with your grandad he got a girl into trouble you
know how it was in those days and her parents didn't want
them to get married so there was a disgrace this was in Flint
North Wales and your grandad well he didn't know what
to do so he decided to go out to India and get a job in the
steel industry there in somewhere called Jam-something let
me look it up, oh yes, Jamshedpur and that's where he met
your grandma. Now she was well to do as they say and they
owned farms in Wigan. Gill family. That's why you and your
dad both have that name so they went out to India and that's
where your grandparents met I don't think they knew each
other for long but they got married and then went down to
Australia but your dad always says that he only lived there
for a few months and then never saw his dad again it's very
sad isn't it but your grandmother was a difficult woman very
proud woman anyway after a bit of time in India I don't
know how long they ended up back in Cheshire, Padgate I
think, and like I said your dad never saw his dad again his
mum told him that his dad died terrible isn't it all those years
they could've been in touch and even met up but your dad
thought his dad was dead I think it's a disgrace apparently he used to get letters from him from Australia but your
grandma opened them and never let your dad see them it
wasn't until you were about to be born that they got in touch

families in those days it was all about appearances I don't like a lot about the modern times but at least we can be honest about families and stuff like that anyway your dad was too young to be in the main army but he joined the home guard and then he was in the Irish Fusiliers and then he was in Palestine after the war and Alexandria he told me but you know he didn't like to speak a lot about himself and then he was back in Wales living in that big house on the hill it's a nursing home now I always thought it was haunted but then your grandma's sister Renee used to do the Ouija board and speak to the dead she was a weird one never married anyway he was in Wales and we were in Wales I've told you that haven't I we were evacuated from Liverpool in 1940 bombs dropping near our back garden in Mossley Hill we were thrown out of bed one night there was such a bang your grandad decided it was safer to move away so we went to Prestatyn and your mum and me we went to Rhyl grammar school had all our lessons in Welsh it was so difficult at first as we didn't know a word oh it's so many years ago now but your mum and dad they married at the Methodist church your dad was very dashing and had all the girls after him I never liked him that much at the time to be honest he was too I don't know well *charming* you know used to turn up at the front door carrying a red rose for your mum with his hair slicked back and always wearing a tie and there was me in my pinnie and my hair a mess.

Yes, your dad did quite a bit of research about the Houghs he was quite an intellectual not like me haha he said you were related to the Cromwells not the one with a statue in

Warrington what's his name Oliver but the other one you know that book was written about him recently by somebody mantelpiece wasn't it or something like that anyway it won some big prize. That's right I've got some notes about this your dad gave me hang on . . . er *Thomas* Cromwell that's the one. Well his daughter married a Hough and they lived near Chester not far from where you were born. Let me get me glasses . . . okay here we are this is what your dad wrote:

King Henry VIII's right-hand man, Thomas Cromwell, had an illegitimate daughter, Jane, born to an unknown mother while he was mourning the loss of his wife and daughters. In 1539 Cromwell's records show him paying for clothing and expenses for Jane, and she ended up marrying William Hough of Leighton (now Neston), Wirral, Cheshire, around 1550. William Hough was the son of Richard Hough who was Cromwell's agent in Chester from 1534 to 1540. Rather astonishingly, as Thomas Cromwell probably did more than anyone else to implement the physical enforcement of the Reformation in England, Jane and her husband were staunch Roman Catholics. They, together with their daughter, Alice, and her husband, William Whitmore, and their children, all came to the attention of the authorities as recusants during the reign of Elizabeth I. William actually spent the last four years of his life in prison for refusing to give up his Catholic faith. Jane was buried on 3 November 1580 near the family home in Neston, which is around an hour's walk from where Stephen was born in Heswall. Or change directions, and in the same amount of time you could walk to Thornton Hough where, in *c*.1300 Ellen de Thornton was born who later married Richard 'Hogh' and whose nuptial union appears to have changed the name of a village which remains to this day. There were Houghs recorded in that part of Cheshire as early as 1260.

Ooh I'm dizzy reading all those long words, I think I'll make a cup of tea.

## The pink moustache

'Will you shave it off when you're fifty? Go on, Dad!' Little did I know that he would not live many years beyond that naked upper lip, but I did suspect that he would begin to grow it again the day after the razor's assault.

My father always had a moustache. But even in my early years it had already became greyish when his hair was still blackish; then one day it was pink. Hilbre Lodge, Ladies' Night, the once-a-year event for the Worshipful Master (my father that year): he must look smart, dinner jacket pressed, hair neatly parted, shirt crisp, eye ready for the ladies, light on in the bathroom, leaning forward, eyes wide open, unscrew the bottle, black goo, concentrate, apply carefully, head turned to the side, and back, and up to the ceiling, a smile of satisfaction under the jet-black lip. Ronald Colman lives again.

But an hour later the black had turned to a purply pink: the man with the pink moustache. What the hell . . . my eyes blurring with tears of laughter. 'It's pink, Dad, it's pink!' He rushes up to the bathroom, ferocious scrubbing, water, soap, water, soap, rubbing left to right, right to left, we're late, eyes craning to see, swirls of purply dye swilling down the plughole, more soaping, we're late, more rinsing. In the end it was a greyish pink, almost the sort of hair colour that ladies who lunch in Palm Beach pay much to achieve – their moustaches already tweezed or waxed away.

## Heads up: Three tricks my father taught me

About to enter a darkened room? Close one eye outside, then release as you go inside.

About to sneeze? Press firmly where nose meets upper lip.

About to sleep? Consciously relax tongue, resting tip against bottom teeth.

## Posthumous poet

I recently found a poem in my father's papers, published in an Open University magazine. I think it conveys keenly his sense of time running out (he only lived a year beyond writing it) and of opportunities lost. But the last two, defiant lines have an almost Nietzschean flash of confidence about them, albeit with a smaller moustache.

### Thursday's Child

*Restlessness! Within me before birth.*
*Bequeathed perhaps by some far distant*
*traveller*
*So that his quest goes on.*

*How restless now? Now that horizon closes*
*in before the search is ended.*
*Signposts swing away: the roads become*
*tracks; and my stride is less sure.*
*My sickness – for such it has become –*
*twists mind and body.*
*The animal looks wildly for a path to*
*run along.*
*A blind running: for nothing: to nothing.*

*No panic shows; but behind, a dead-of-night,*
*dark, desperation –*
*Not that I shall fail.*
*But that I shall succeed alone.*

## The pianos I've owned

My first piano has already been described – the German
rosewood upright, bought in a Stockton Heath antique shop
for £5. I remember its richly grained case with two candlestick holders and (eighty-five) yellow, ivory keys – and only

two pedals, the right-hand one of which was worn down to a shiny brassy smoothness. And I've written about the piano before that, the blue-painted toy piano bought when my pestering had worn down my parents: 'That'll keep him quiet' was the unspoken implication.

Moving on a year or so, my second proper piano was a Danemann six-foot grand, English-made, bought (at a great discount due to the shop manager's generosity) from Dawson's in Warrington. This was the store where we bought all our records but sometimes I would go along just to play their instruments. When I tried this Danemann, with its walnut case containing so many more colours and possibilities than my upright at home, my eyes opened wide with delight. And it was a *grand* – a proper piano. Later we bought a blond-coloured Ibach, the same size but a lightweight, ditzy piano with a lightweight action. It was grander than the Danemann but I always thought it had a more inflated sense of its own beauty than was deserved. Its skittish, shallow keys were not good for me in those muscle-developing, reflex-forming years. It was eventually sold to buy my first black piano – a solid, shiny Yamaha, again from Dawson's. This piano was a companion for many hard-working years. I came to musical and pianistic maturity on it and it travelled with me to New York when I signed my first lease on my first post-student apartment, in Washington Heights. It may well still be making music in an American home somewhere.

When my father died in 1982 he left me a little money with which to buy my first Steinway, a seven-foot 'B'. I still have this lovely instrument and I expect to die with it in my possession. After that a mellow Steinway 'B' from the 1920s, later bought from me by my friend, the pianist Stephen Coombs. Then a dazzling, edgy, New York Steinway 'L' which had been a rehearsal piano at the Marlboro Music Festival in the early 1980s and which was in my Manhattan apartment, but which has now emigrated to London. And over the years . . . an old Bechstein eight-foot, delicate in sound but with a case as heavy as a tank; two singing and soulful pre-war six-foot Blüthners; a brand new Fazioli seven-foot bought from the factory in Italy – a brief affair; an ancient, battered Grotrian-Steinweg; a even more ancient Tomkison square (for use as a desk on which to paint); an 1880s six-foot Chickering, now at home in St Thomas Choir School in New York. But never yet a concert grand, a 'D', a nine-foot, full-size piano. My life, my tool . . . but only on stage.

## *The Dream of Gerontius*

'What's this?' barked my composition teacher, Douglas Steele, as he struck the twelve chords which accompany the Priest's majestic opening declamation ('Proficiscere, anima Christiana') in Elgar's *The Dream of Gerontius*. They were played as always by Douglas with his sumptuous tone, scooped out of the upright piano like *boules* of dense vanilla ice cream. 'I don't know, Mr Steele.' 'Well, it's *The Dream of Gerontius* by Sir Edward Elgar, my boy. Go and listen to it, and study it.

Words of Cardinal Newman.' Rather than go to the library I walked up Deansgate to Forsyths, the music shop, to buy the blue Novello vocal score and the EMI boxed set of Barbirolli conducting the Hallé Orchestra – angelic Janet Baker singing the Angel, Richard Lewis matchless in the title role, and Kim Borg saving the recording from perfection by his lamentably bad English pronunciation. Despite that flaw, it's still one of the greatest recordings made of anything.

I wore out the vinyl discs and to this day I can't hear 'Be merciful' without hearing this recording's muffled Manchester cough deep in the lungs of the strings' striding counterpoint, from a member of the chorus perhaps – bronchitis was common in smoky northern British towns and cities in 1965. It was recorded in the Free Trade Hall, where they would still have had ashtrays in the auditorium at that time – Woodbines stubbed out between the seats during performances. In filmed footage of this orchestra we can see the players themselves smoking during rehearsals, much as today they might sip from a plastic bottle of designer water.

*Gerontius* (or *The Dream* in Barbirolli's quirky diminutive) changed my life. It was literally my first step towards Catholicism, which in itself was my first step towards discipline and serenity in my turbulent mid-teens. From the Victorian chapel in Dover Road and my white-bread, white-skinned, tinned Cheshire life, my world began to blossom. Joseph, pray for me. Mary, pray for me. Purgatory, Masses, angels, saints . . . it seemed as naughty to me aged fourteen as checking out volumes of Henry Miller at Warrington Public Library.

'I will never speak to you again if you become a Catholic,' said my desperate grandmother. But on 14 September 1980 she embraced me after the Mass when I was received into the Catholic Church. This woman, who grew up in a Liverpool where Catholics and Protestants used to throw stones at each other, was not about to join me, but the kindness and warmth of Fr Maurus Green OSB, my instructor and the celebrant that evening at St Mary's, Buttermarket Street, Warrington, won her over. I brought her back a rosary from Fatima a few years later and she took it from me with a sly smile ('my mother would turn in her grave'). The next time we visited her it was hanging on the mantelpiece above the chimney. There was more holiness in her gentle acceptance and tolerance than in my proselytising. I wonder now, as my Catholicism has changed shape, whether I would be as full of grace if someone gave me a rosary from Fatima?

## On stage

Strangely enough, until the final stages of writing this book, I'd completely forgotten about a number of concerts I played whilst a student at Chetham's. There was my concerto debut with the Stockport Youth Orchestra playing Mozart K414. Then a little later, Mendelssohn First with the Liverpool Mozart Players, followed by the same piece (just the second and third movements) with the Hallé Orchestra and James Loughran at the Free Trade Hall on Valentine's Day 1974. There were also recitals along the way – in Rhyl, Crosby,

Chester, Crewe and other places reasonably close to home. There are tapes somewhere, recorded by my father on a chunky Grundig reel-to-reel machine. But it's puzzling that it was only when this book was in the hands of the publisher, and I was sifting through memories once more to ensure accuracy, that this public activity of my early life which became my professional life came to light, to life again. Had it been pushed to the back of my mind deliberately or had other things simply jostled their way to the front?

To this day I sometimes think, when standing in the wings of a large concert hall thousands of miles from where I was born (usually with a smile of affection): how did I get here? Who are all those people out there? Wouldn't it be better for me to be hidden away in my old bedroom in All Saints Drive, a joss stick fogging the air? Sometimes, I confess, very occasionally, I've played something faster than I intended to, not so as to catch the last train but to abscond from the embarrassment of sharing further private intimacies with the public. Playing in front of an audience is not terrifying just because of the physical or mental demands. A greater challenge can be this revealing of ourselves to strangers, this inviting the public into our purple bedrooms. There are times when we just want to lock the door from inside and hide away. Unless we're writing a memoir, I suppose . . .

# RNCM

# Leaving Chetham's

Six O levels. Two grade As (Music and English Literature), three Bs (English Language, French and Religious Studies) and a C in History. At the mock exams, a few months earlier, my grade in Maths (19 per cent) was deemed too low to be worth the price of the examination paper. If I agreed to undergo coaching they said they would let me take it. But I was sick of Chetham's by then and, due to a stroke of luck and some of the best advice Gordon Green ever gave me, I decided to leave school early and go to the Royal Northern College of Music. Gordon had sensed my unhappiness, he saw my underachievement, and he managed to persuade the authorities at the RNCM to allow me to begin my degree two years early, two months shy of my sixteenth birthday, with no A levels. Chets and I had served each other badly. I entered with an eleven-plus pass, a love for the piano, a first prize in the Thelwall County Primary egg and spoon race, and an enthusiasm for the exciting new life to come in Manchester in my bright blue school uniform. I left introverted, afraid, bored and grossly underachieving. Of course, adolescence played a part in the dysfunction, but too often Chetham's was, in the 1970s, unlike now, a place to be unhappy – and many were.

But then something sparked into life when I entered the RNCM. Partly it was the fact that I was able to go there at all. Gordon Green and Clifton Helliwell (head of keyboard) had pressed for it to happen; both saw something in me beneath the surface scratches.

But two further things happened in my first year of study there that would change my life: I took part in (and won the piano section of) the first BBC Young Musician competition; and I attended my first ever Mass, leading to my conversion to Catholicism.

## A fabulous zigzag run

In my first term at the RNCM a new competition was to take place: BBC Young Musician of the Year. I thought it would be exciting to enter although Gordon Green, as mentioned earlier, was deeply sceptical about all such gladiatorial tournaments. I suppose this particular competition didn't seem that serious as it was aimed at those too young to embark on a professional career, and so, with a tolerant sigh and weary resignation, he agreed to let me enter. It was something to work for, to gain experience, perhaps even have fun . . . whatever.

My memory is blank about most of it but I do remember the final two solo rounds taking place in the concert hall of the RNCM. I played Bach, Busoni and Bach-Busoni in the semis (I liked the literary symmetry as much as the music itself), and then for the finals just one piece: the Liszt B minor Sonata. I know there was some controversy about my winning first prize and I remember something in the jurors' announcement about there actually being a tie for first place with myself and Paul Coker, and that the judges were split down the middle, and no one would agree to change their vote, and only because I was younger would I be awarded the prize. It was all a bit of a fumble. I thought everyone was better than me anyway – Jeremy Atkin's scintillating Chopin Scherzo, Barry Douglas's thrilling Liszt Legend, Paul Coker's brilliant Tippett Second Sonata (I knew that piece) – so I really just wanted to go home and watch *Coronation Street*.

But I was given the first prize and went through to the concerto finals. My original choice had been Brahms's Second, the longest and most challenging concerto in the pianist's repertoire. I loved the piece and had worked quite a lot on it, but I chickened out. I'd been invited to play Mozart K449 in a concert later that year and so, having it in my fingers, I offered it instead. It was a bizarre decision. Even in a competition actually requiring a Mozart concerto this slender work would be an unlikely choice – and then I chickened out of playing it from memory too. I remembering warming up an hour before I was due to go on stage (I think it was in Gordon Green's studio) and the other piano finalists coming along to wish me well. 'Gosh, I find this passage so tricky,' I said, partly out of genuine nervousness but more as a kind of apology that I was about to perform rather than one of them. I played the beginning of the zigzag run at the end of the first movement cadenza to point out the bit I meant. One of my fellow competitors leant over and looked at the score then placed his fingers on the keyboard, zipping through

163

it perfectly, his fingers fluid and fabulous. Actually I don't think it was a mean gesture, and I didn't take it as such at the time, but it alerted me to real life at a music college. No, there were to be no razor blades between the keys, as legend had it, but competitions are not just held in public. They can happen over a cup of coffee, or in a practice studio with a fabulous zigzag run.

## Doors opening

I had some superb teachers at the RNCM. I can't list exactly what I learned from each one, but some things stick in my mind. They opened doors . . .

Colin Beeson – 'Beethoven was not the first Romantic composer. He was always a classicist.' Yes, an invaluable point of reference when playing his works.

Douglas Jarman – 'hexachordal combinatoriality'. I still love that phrase and I ended up referencing this serial technique in my Piano Sonata III (*Trinitas*). Little did we know, when he was teaching us callow, first-year students the fundamentals of the Second Viennese School (Webern, didn't he write *Invitation to the Dance*?), that Douglas was a world authority on Alban Berg and one of the main editors for the revised Universal Edition of his works.

Michel Brandt – tight curly hair, dapper French accent, ear acute as a whippet. *Solfège* (it was much more) in highest Grade 5 often consisted of listening to a snippet of a recording of a complex score (something like Schoenberg's

*Variations for Orchestra*) and having to write down whatever we could hear.

David Fanning – also *solfège*, a younger Michel Brandt without the curly hair or the French accent . . . but with an even sharper ear. He also played the piano superbly. I heard him perform Prokofiev's Third Concerto with the college orchestra and, at a recital somewhere in Manchester, the B minor *Etude Tableau* of Rachmaninov, the repeated notes perfectly spat out and rhythm sharp as a tack.

Sir William Glock – 'I read a little Homer before I go to sleep.' Probably in Greek. We took Beethoven's Trio op. 1 no. 3 to our chamber music lessons and I remember intuiting for the first time from his rigorous comments that harmonic surprise or ambiguity could have architectural implications, not just emotional ones. Did he always wear that dove-grey suit with a bottle-green knitted tie? Was he still Mr BBC Classical Music at that point? Was he still the UK's arbiter of new music, banning twentieth-century composers who deviated from a high-Modernist orthodoxy? He was unfailingly charming, disarmingly impressive with a sort of suave, immovable confidence: public school, Cambridge, the RAF, the BBC. He was not alone on that elite path in British musical life at that time.

Sir John Manduell – 'You should have a good holiday, but I think you're more a fjords man than lounging on a beach.' The principal's comment to me after my last busy six days at college, playing a recital, Rachmaninov's Second with the Hallé Orchestra and, fear overcome, Brahms's Second with the college orchestra. (He was wrong about the fjords though.) South African Sir John gave Sir William a run for his rand in the confident commander department, with his easy smile cast around freely and a breezy authority in his assured gait and upright spine – even if his pale safari suits and smouldering Gitanes lacked the ultimate aplomb of Sir William's Savile Row assurance. He would probably have been more fun over a bottle of wine, though.

Vlado Perlemuter – 'Don't play it like Meyerbeer.' If only I'd known that composer's operas better. At the time I barely knew his name. There was a list pinned up on the School of Keyboard noticeboard of the repertoire Perlemuter would teach in his regular masterclasses: all of Chopin, all of Ravel, and then a select list of other composers and their works, including Franck's *Prélude, Choral et Fugue* which had drawn that critical comment when I brought it to him. He taught nothing Russian as I recall, although I did play him the first movement of Rachmaninov's Second Concerto when we had some time left over once. He almost blushed as he told me that this was not his kind of music. Still, he listened and was appreciative, although he had no suggestions to make. He was always quiet when teaching these classes, sometimes virtually inaudible as he made his comments, scribbling fingerings in the score in ink, and pulling his scarf around his neck.

Eli Goren – this founding first violinist of the Allegri String Quartet was my first taste of pre-war, middle European, Jewish musical tradition. My friend Sara Norwood studied with him and I would go along to her lessons to play most weeks. I was charmed by his thick Viennese accent, which somehow breathed music. As he picked up the violin to demonstrate it seemed like an embrace, as if the instrument were a child being carried tenderly to safety.

There were two distinguished cellist-teachers: firstly the head of strings, Eleanor Warren, nightly propping up the college bar with a series of gin and tonics and an ashtray overflowing with cigarette butts. Voice gravelly as a stubbed-out Marlboro. And, along the same bar, there leant Terence Weil with his shaky hands and kind Cockney-tinged voice, and also his constant smoking – Players Weights though, non-filter, stashed in great cartons in his briefcase. Much coughing too. Always much coughing in Manchester.

One of its most famous visiting coughers was the most famous musical Pole. As we stand with Eleanor and Terry, and look back from the bar, pointing a cigarette slightly to the right, there you can see a statue of Chopin, near the original front entrance of the RNCM, up the stone staircase, in the window – a larger-than-life bronze likeness for such a diminutive man. It's a wonderful piece by Ludwika Nitschowa, given to the college in 1973 by the Fryderyk Chopin Society of Poland. The composer looks almost Byronic, despite clutching a muffler to his neck against the chills of northern England. It commemorates the visit he made to Manchester on 25 August 1848 (after an eight-hour journey from Edinburgh) to play a concert three days later. Within a year he was dead. Malaga might have been a better choice.

## One of the greatest men I've met

Studies with Gordon Green continued for my first year at the RNCM until he became sick, and then I went to Derrick Wyndham. Derrick was chalk to Gordon's cheese – a shy, intense, strict, even repressed man whose comments could be rapier sharp. Gordon's baggy tweed jacket or fisherman's smocks could not be imagined on Derrick, who always wore a sharply tailored suit, his silk tie held in place by a chained clip. Gordon's goatee could never have grown on Derrick's handsome, smooth face with its enigmatic, hard-to-fathom smile. Derrick was a man with nothing out of place, every tooth (real ones in contrast to Gordon's dentures) seemingly individually polished.

He had the reputation of being a technician to Gordon's musician, but this was one of those meaningless generalisations. It's true that Gordon had little enthusiasm for teaching systematic technique and he let me get away with much sloppiness. I think his reasoning was that I would sort out the problems for myself, and that a simple passage in that Mozart slow movement would take a life to get right, so why waste precious time worrying about a mechanical deficiency here or an inaccuracy there? He was not uninterested (early on he introduced me to the Pischna scale exercise and encouraged me to work on Joseffy exercises) but he wanted to think pure 'music' as a conductor or composer might think it.

I'd studied with Gordon for around seven years so it was time for a change anyway, but Derrick was a bracing one.

On occasion I would finish playing a piece, perhaps with more bravado than bravura, and he would look at me with a quizzical smile on his face, head slightly tipped at an angle: 'Well, you can't play it like *that* in a concert or a recording.' I remember once, when I was about to play him a Chopin étude, he sat close to the piano: 'If you drop one note there's not much point in playing it really. Okay, go ahead.' He was not a tyrant, and everything was said calmly with precision and politeness, but it was certainly intimidating at times.

But I learned so much from him and carry his ideas with me every time I practise or play, passing them on to every student I teach. 'The geography of the keyboard' was a concept of his I found hugely helpful – the layout of the notes and the negotiation the hand (and arm) has to make to travel across their terrain. He understood the connection fingers have to keys with a clarity I have not encountered since. And technique matters: the greatest musician on earth cannot make the close of Beethoven's final piano sonata float to heaven if she cannot trill properly.

Derrick's teachers had been Artur Schnabel and Moriz Rosenthal (a tiny, signed photo of the latter hung on the wall of Room 426 where he always taught) and this contrast of totally different styles, students of Leschetizky and Liszt respectively, served him well. He, like Gordon, never demonstrated but once I remember him telling me to practise scales in sixths (an especially awkward technical feat) and, sitting at the right of the keyboard, he leant over and dashed off such a scale with unbelievable virtuosity and aplomb. My eyes widened with astonishment, but then he retreated back into his English gentleman's shell. Or was he actually English?

The rumours were manifold – he was Polish, he'd been a child prodigy, he'd been a prisoner of war, he'd spent days floating in the ocean . . . and so on. Late in his life, when he'd retired to Bognor Regis, I went to meet him for lunch in the hope of finding out something about his life before he began teaching at the RNCM. We had a prawn cocktail in one of those uniquely English hotels, a fancier Fawlty Towers, and chatted pleasantly about this and that, dabbing our lips with the pink paper napkins. I tried to steer the conversation to deeper topics but . . . somehow he took hold of the wheel and we were back in a more mundane direction as we buttered our bread rolls from tiny sachets of Anchor butter, seagulls cawing outside.

Eventually I asked a more direct question and he braced himself. I took out my mental pen and paper and prepared to jot down the revelation to come. But it didn't. He'd been ill after the war, he said, and after recovering in hospital his doctor told him that he shouldn't play concerts any more but should teach instead. 'Part of my recovery was not to dwell on the past so that's all I can say really.' And so the china pots of Nescafé arrived and the bill, and I went back to the train station. Earlier, when I'd been studying with him, he told me that he'd recorded many 78s (in Italy) but that they'd been destroyed in the war. Possessions, achievements, families . . . destroyed in the war. Such a common theme for those who emerged alive if not unscathed after the barbaric twentieth-century conflicts.

And then, just a few months ago, when these reminiscences were pretty much finished, I got an email from one of his former students who had been in touch with the daughter-in-law of one of Derrick's closest friends. Mystery solved. His real name was Bronislaw Hankowski, born in 1921. He shows up playing recitals at the Schubert-Saal of the Konzerthaus in Vienna on both 6 and 15 February 1933 with ambitious repertoire including the Bach/Tausig Toccata and Fugue in D minor, Liszt's Second Polonaise and 'La Campanella' Etude, and three of his own compositions. (Curiously on the same day in the Mozart-Saal of the same Konzerthaus a certain Arnold Schoenberg was giving a lecture at exactly the same time.) Then he appears in documents held at Southampton University as the recipient of a grant in 1935–8 from the Education Aid Society, an organisation that helped Jewish children; and later it appears he joined the RAF in 1941 in Padgate. Then the curtain is drawn and he reinvents himself with a changed name: an English gentleman in Bowdon, Cheshire.

He lived there in a beautiful Victorian house shared with Frederic Cox, the former principal of, and professor of singing at, the Royal Manchester College of Music, later changed to Royal Northern. They were two bachelors who shared their post-war lives in this elegant suburb. (An eight-minute walk down the street had lived Hans Richter in his Hallé years, the conductor of the premieres of Wagner's *Ring* and

Brahms's Second Symphony, and around the corner had been born John Ireland.) I went to Derrick's house for dinner once and it was surprisingly . . . pink. I remember curtsying ornaments and pretty lace and cute chintz, not the expected decor for a house where two unmarried gentlemen lived. Of course, many came to *that* conclusion. But not only, during a brief tour before dinner, did Derrick point out his separate wing of the house to Freddy's, but they addressed each other throughout the evening as Mr Cox and Mr Wyndham. And then, not so many years before he died, Derrick married one of Freddy's students, Sylvia Jacobs. And the three of them lived happily ever after in the elegant house in Bowdon. Until Freddy died and Derrick retired, then it was Bognor Regis. And the starchy bread rolls. And the tiny sachets of Anchor butter as the seagulls cawed.

'It was not the plan,' he told me with a sardonic edge. 'I intended to move to the south of France when I left the college but . . . well, the exchange rate and . . .' His voice trailed off and his life trailed off. He'd never been able to continue the playing career which had started so precociously but he had survived the war, whatever the war had meant to him in personal suffering. And he had taught generations of young pianists. Some over the years have told me how much he made them suffer through his sarcastic remarks and impossible-to-please perfectionism. 'I was terrified of Derrick Wyndham,' said one, when asked about his lessons. But I never saw that side of him and I treasure his memory as one of the greatest men I've met.

## Composing and orchards

My move to the RNCM had countless positives, except one: I could not continue my composition studies. Teaching composition is a waste of time on one level. Theory, harmony, counterpoint, orchestration, score-reading, music history, *solfège*, playing an instrument . . . yes. All invaluable to a composer, and I continued studying these as part of my general musical education. But in the end all an actual composition teacher can do is to encourage or discourage, point out what he or she would or wouldn't do, plus the discipline of weekly lessons to keep the student's creative fire burning.

So I was left to write by myself. And I did – organ music, a flute sonata, more piano pieces, more songs and then, at Juilliard, where there was a similar ban on pianists studying composition, I wrote the only surviving and published piece from my early years: a viola sonata. It had begun life as a trombone sonata (a request from a student), then had a brief fling as a cello sonata before finding its vocation up an octave.

Then, after years of encouraging teachers, a discouraging colleague in New York entered my life. I showed this student some music I'd written and she dismissed it as being of no merit or interest. 'Stick to the piano,' she said. And so I did. After winning the Naumburg Competition in 1983 there was little time to do anything but be *stuck* to the piano. But just as a little boost of confidence can be a seed starting an orchard, so its opposite can be like cutting a ring around the bark of a tree. I wrote many transcriptions as encore pieces over the next fifteen years but very little of my own music. Composition became a memory from a distant past. But then, in the mid-1990s, I was hanging out with the composer John Corigliano, having just given a recital at Alice Tully Hall in New York. As an encore I'd played my arrangement of the *Carousel Waltz* and he took me aside backstage and said, 'I really liked it, Stephen. Why don't you write your own music? It basically just means using your material rather than Richard Rodgers's.' A seed . . . an orchard.

## A screech in the library

The library at the RNCM was not large, but if anything was missing, just down the road was the Henry Watson Music Library, one of the oldest and most extensive public collections in the world. It's strange to think now how thrilling was the sense of discovery running fingers along shelf after shelf of spines, eventually to prise one desired volume out from the rest. Today even phones allow us to search with ease and then download whatever book or score we want, but in the old libraries it was as if that special book was looking for us. *God in Search of Man*, as Rabbi Abraham Joshua Heschel's book title has it. Humans are browsers more than surfers. To browse is to find nourishment; to surf is to skim on top. We are creatures of land not sea.

With listening libraries, though, it's hard to make any case for the old ways being superior. Before CDs we had to check out or listen on site to LPs and put up with previous borrowers' fingerprints or scratches, every new hearing involving a small, incremental destruction. Nevertheless, I remember two revelatory occasions at the RNCM when actually seeing the physical twelve-inch sleeves in the display troughs meant that I donned the headphones, dropped the needle and listened, pinned to the chair with life-changing astonishment.

I'd become obsessed with Wagner after discovering *Gerontius* and I bought sets of most of his operas – my gold, Deutsche Grammophon Karajan *Ring* almost needed a wheelbarrow for delivery, so heavy was the thick box with its fat book alongside the many vinyl platters. From there to Richard Strauss was an obvious progression, and looking through the library's opera section I came across the screeching cover of Georg Solti's *Elektra*, Birgit Nilsson wild and mad in the photograph. Who could resist? I grabbed a score, placed the first LP on the turntable and carefully rested the needle into the outer grooves. Then I stopped breathing . . . before I began hyperventilating. I'd never heard anything like this.

Then a different discovery – Ervin Nyiregyházi. I'd read something at the time about his new Liszt release, and about his uniquely bizarre life story: from child prodigy in Budapest to homeless person in San Francisco, chanced upon by a record producer as he played a concert in a church to help finance medical care for one of his ten wives. He'd apparently not practised for decades but now here was someone playing like no one else, allowing the listener to rediscover a lost world which it seemed had disappeared for ever. I was not responding to a publicist's hype when I had the impression that Liszt himself had been reincarnated. The first track, *Aux cyprès de la Villa d'Este*, thundered into my headphones and I shuddered with a kind of recognition. It felt like I'd been transported to Weimar and was in the company of Liszt, not because of any technical brilliance (there was none) but because in the depths of that clangorous piano's bass octaves in the RNCM library that day I felt I'd found the very source of the composer's soul, its profound spiritual rapture, its tugging, sagging melancholy.

## Devon and the Tiber

Seeds of interest in Catholicism were sown early, despite my suspicions as an evangelical. Nicholas Ashton was one of the first people I met who was both intelligent and interested in Catholicism, and I was intrigued by the rosary beads that tumbled out of his school trousers. He told me he used to incense them, and they certainly cast a strange, alluring perfume around him. Then there was *The Dream of Gerontius* from my mid-teens when I became intoxicated by the music of Elgar and fascinated by Cardinal Newman and his conversion.

But the match was actually struck at Buckfast Abbey. I was in Devon in August 1978 to play a concert at Dartington Summer School at the invitation of its founder and director, Sir William Glock, who was also my chamber music coach at the RNCM. I was to play Mozart's Piano Concerto K449 (debuted at the BBC competition earlier that year, with its tricky, zigzag run), and my mother and I were staying at a bed and breakfast close by, the owners of which happened to be Catholics. Pope Paul VI had recently died and his funeral was showing on the television set in the main lounge – it was 12 August. The multitudes gathered in Rome and the intense sound of the voices singing the plangent music astonished me – I'd never even seen a Catholic Mass before, never mind a requiem for a pope. A mere ten-minute walk down the road was Buckfast Abbey, the Benedictine monastery. One afternoon I wandered inside the main church and was entranced by . . . something. There was a warmth within, a serenity, a Presence – I can't fully explain it. There was a little shrine at the back with a photograph of the late pope where people had lit candles and were praying for the repose of his soul. I was at the very point of stopping going to church completely. I was sick of Sundays at Dover Road and there wasn't anywhere else I wanted to go. I was sixteen and my past religious observance seemed like something cumbersome from childhood to shake off. My voice had broken. I was shaving. It was time to give up church-going.

But I went to Mass that Sunday with my mother, no idea what was going on, my first encounter with a Catholic building – I'd not yet travelled to continental Europe. When we got home I sought out Catholic churches in the area, exploring on my moped, and starting with weekly Mass at Our Lady's in Latchford before moving to St Mary's in Buttermarket Street, Warrington. I'd been told the latter had a strong musical tradition and their sung 11 a.m. Latin Mass turned out to be quite wonderful, with a dedicated choir and Benedictine priests celebrating. It was there I met Fr Maurus Green.

My third year at the RNCM (1979–80) was filled with Mass attendance; I went every lunchtime to the Catholic chaplaincy at Holy Name Church close by. I received Communion daily but couldn't make the final plunge of actually converting. I didn't want to go to Confession (a mere temperamental blip), but more seriously I still didn't believe all the teachings. I had problems with some Marian doctrines and certain sacramental issues, in particular 'intention' and its relation to consecration, whether of Host or priest. I was coming from a literalist background at Dover Road, and although I did see how unhistorical their fundamentalist interpretation of Scripture was, I still carried with me the need to see an idea logically through to its end, regardless of the poetic deviations which can make doctrines hold wine if not water.

My eyes eventually opened to the idea that, as G. K. Chesterton pointed out, a myth can contain more *truth* than a fact; it can be broader, deeper, more flexible and more historically telling. The Book of Genesis recounts the story of the creation of the world in seven days. To understand this literally is nonsense; to understand it symbolically (life emerging in stages) is an early prophecy of evolutionary theory. So far no dispute. But if Catholic theology tells us that Mary is the Mediatrix of all Grace how could St Paul, the Apostle of Grace, fail even to mention her name in his New Testament writings? It's not that we should expect the writers of the first century to think with the same set of parameters as we do (that's another fundamentalism), but omission to include something can be as significant as its inclusion. Nevertheless I eventually pushed these doubts aside and made the move.

Theological problems along these lines remain for me today but, unlike now, then I was fanatically Catholic. I accepted the One True Church trope; I affirmed the traditional statement that all those who were not in communion with the Pope of Rome were either heretics or infidels. I devoured a huge tome, *The Catechism Explained*, bought for pennies at McGill's second-hand bookshop near the university. I spent many hours in the back of this shop leafing through theological volumes from earlier times, most of them thrown out of convent libraries when Vatican II's spring clean was at its zenith. This one, around eight hundred pages crammed with bracing certainties, had a publication date of 1899, the highpoint of the sort of Catholicism where every doubt had been vanquished and every question had a clear answer.

But all of this (and what was to come) aside: my conversion to Catholicism completely and utterly turned my life around. From a TV-binging borderline depressive I became intellectually curious, hard-working, disciplined, concerned about others and, above all, joyful.

## Living as a priest in Manchester

After a couple of years commuting from Warrington to Manchester on the train (fears of being mugged now vanquished), and having bought a perky green Morris Minor for £200 from the two tweeded ladies of Irby, Margaret and Ethel Bell, it seemed a good time to leave home and move into a flat in Manchester. We hadn't even begun scouring the small ads, the student noticeboards or the estate agents when my mother met up with a friend of a friend whose boy was attending St Bede's College, an independent Catholic boys' school on Alexandra Road South in Whalley Range. 'They rent out rooms there, I believe,' said the woman to my mother. 'Here's the rector's phone number. You should get Stephen to give him a call.' As a fervent Catholic this seemed like the perfect solution – to live in an institution with priests and a chapel, not far from the RNCM. I picked up the phone and dialled the number. 'Monsignor Dodgeon here.' 'Hello Monsignor. Forgive me for calling you out of the blue but Mrs N. gave me your number and she said I should phone. She said you have rooms to rent. I'm a student at the Royal Northern and I'm looking for a place to live near the college. Oh, and I became a Catholic recently.' 'Ah well, no, we don't take in lodgers I'm afraid. I really don't—' 'Oh, I forgot to mention, I think I may have a vocation to the priesthood.' There was a short pause and his voice changed. 'Ah, let me see. Perhaps we *can* find somewhere.' He did, and I spent a couple of happy years living in a room along a corridor of priests. My immediate neighbour was retired Fr Patrick Madden.

The story was that he had been ill and so had had to retire from the missions – in South America, I think. I don't know any more about his background but I do know he was a crazy misfit, an IRA apologist and a Latin liturgy obsessive – he hinted that Vatican II was a devilish affair and that Pope John Paul II wasn't really the pope. As a recent convert I was barely even a proper Catholic to him and he was always standoffish, refusing to smile and fixing me with a hard stare. He would sit in his room all day long watching television, leaving only for meals or to tinker with his old car around the back of the buildings – also a green Morris Minor. At this point I thought everything Catholic was true and perfect and beyond criticism so it was quite a shock to be in such close proximity to a priest who was so bitter and damaged. Funnily enough, as the months passed, we actually became friends in a way. I never rose to his bait – he would say something outrageous and then glare at me for a reaction. He would put pamphlets under my door – writings of Malachi Martin were often amongst them. I must have worn him down with kindness, or more likely naivety.

There were other eccentrics there at the time. There was a common bathroom, with two walls of sinks, and I remember one of the priests had a toothbrush that was so worn down I think there were perhaps nine bristles left on it, each barely a centimetre long. There was another priest who loved to watch soap operas. I would go down to the common room, which was next to the television room where he'd be sitting, riveted by the latest episode of *Crossroads*. As it was finishing he'd stand up impatiently: 'Utter rubbish!' he'd say to me, and he'd storm out. A couple of days later I'd be there again and on the screen was Meg Mortimer at the fictional motel's front desk, giving someone the keys to their room or giving instructions to Benny, the handyman. Tony Hatch's A major theme would ring out once more and this priest would stand up once again: 'Utter rubbish!'

I had begun organ lessons at the RNCM with Eric Chadwick, and St Bede's had a small organ in its lovely Italianate chapel, away from the main living quarters. After dinner I would often go down there in the darkness and fire up the two-manual instrument. Lit only by bulbs on the music rack and pedal board, with the red sanctuary light behind me flickering next to the altar's tabernacle, I would practise my César Franck *Trois Chorals*. I don't think you fully 'get' that music unless you have played it shivering in the dark in a cold church, the twisting counterpoint like veins in the marble pillars, the sweet harmonies like last Sunday's incense lingering in the pews. And the radiant climaxes, eruptions of mystical ecstasy, almost need to be experienced alone. *I and thou*: a union needing no audience.

## A vocation to be a pianist

My comment on a vocation on the telephone to Msgr Dodgeon was not false. Twice in my life I've seriously considered leaving the piano behind and becoming a priest. For my mother this would have been the worst possible outcome. Not so much that it seemed like a waste of so many years of work (mine and hers), or that it was a waste of my gifts (the New Testament parable of the man with the talents was often, and inaccurately, quoted to me in those years). No, I think she actually had an allergy towards Catholicism. Buried deep inside her Protestant subconscious was an image of wheedling Irish priests at the bookies, or cruel nuns hitting teenage girls with rulers or . . . that instinctive and illogical aversion which was the result of prejudice from her early years on the streets of tribal Liverpool. Orange and green: unmixable colours.

For me, what was the attraction? No life change as momentous as that has one simple answer. There's no question that a certain kind of Catholicism has a certain kind of attraction for a certain kind of man. Whether it's Oscar Wilde or Gerard Manley Hopkins or Julien Green or Francis Poulenc . . . the list is long. It can be seen as a cauterisation of a wound, the cool of a church after the heat of passion, the sublime replacing the squalor – *ecstasy* indeed, when that literally means standing outside of oneself. (Both 'cloud nine' and 'seventh heaven' are offered as synonyms for that word in a thesaurus I consulted.) Much is on offer in traditional Catholicism, and much delivers. If this is still true in an age when the liturgy is lite and being gay is okay is perhaps debatable; the battle to keep the Latin Mass alive since the reforming 1970s was as much protection as devotion. To kneel at the back of a dark church heavy-laden with statues and stained glass was a tried and trusted road for those with heavy-laden hearts and stained consciences. But that was not the main reason for my interest in religious life, even though avoiding questions about being gay by giving up all sexual activity, identity or marital possibility was a huge plus.

My first stab at entering the priesthood came only months after my conversion (why wait around?). I'd got a scholarship to go to Juilliard but perhaps there was another path. I wrote to the Franciscans explaining my plan for piano studies but that my real desire was to become a priest. 'Go to New York for the two years, then get back in touch,' the novice master wrote back. I was shocked. I thought my youthful ardour and my intended sacrifice would have had them falling over themselves to get me to join the following week, but that wise old father had likely seen many such immature cases over the years. He may have seen through to my vanity, and if he'd told me that the friars were abandoning their habits I would probably have been less interested. If he'd said I'd need to learn the guitar . . . If he'd said I'd need to teach kindergarten . . . If he'd said I'd be posted to Africa . . . I would have given up on them. I wanted a religious order made in my own image.

Obedience in religious life is not so much a matter of the superior's control of the novice but of the novice's curve to learn true freedom. To give up oneself is to receive the gift of being open to the God of Surprises. Nevertheless, I do think my attraction to the priesthood was a genuine one:

to bring joy and comfort to others more than to look for it myself. That unique access a priest has (celibacy has its place here), to go deep down to the most desolate places of human suffering, and not just its physical misery. To offer an ear, a hand, a shoulder; to be a Confessor at the gates of hell.

'Your altar is the piano.' 'There are many priests who are saints. Perhaps not so many pianists' – words from bishops and priests over the years as I was turned away, not because I was unsuitable but because they felt there was another ministry open to me that was of more value. It was a lucky escape in the end because I probably would have been thrown out, or would have walked out. And the piano as an altar? Yes, I like that. Sometimes to this day I whisper to myself, standing in the wings offstage, the concert grand in my sight: 'Introibo ad altare Dei' – I will go to the altar of God. A Jewish psalm. The opening words of the Tridentine Mass. My confession, my confessional.

## The Eighth Day

Most lunchtimes when I was at the RNCM, after attending Mass at the Catholic chaplaincy, I would walk back down Oxford Road to On the Eighth Day, a vegan cafe run as a cooperative on the leftist side of left-wing, all patchouli, old jeans, young beards, political protest and . . . superb, home-made food. It was founded in 1970 and has grown (up) from the most radical roots to its present-day trendier sobriety, but it's still serving delicious food. It used to be a place of confrontation and grunge, but now people peck at iPhones whilst sipping their smoothies.

In their earlier years they had absolutely no dairy, but you could moisten your buckwheat flapjack with some 'cashew-nut cream', a liquefied substance of indeterminate flavour and colour. Those old craggy, gnarled, fibrous flapjacks would, in the pre-Thatcher years, have been merely grazed with carob, whereas now they wear their smothered chocolate coating like a luxuriant cashmere scarf. Herbal tea used to be the only alternative to fruit juice, but now macchiatos froth and sputter from EU-made stainless-steel machines. A range of trendy footwear now walks the floors whereas dried-out open-toe sandals seemed to be de rigueur for the staff back then.

My lunches often finished with my wandering into the radical bookshop next door, Grass Roots, shelves packed with Communist publications, translated and printed in Russia or China. I bought the *Little Red Book* of Chairman Mao one day whilst digesting a nut-roast bake (all I remember from it is the term 'paper tiger') and I often leafed through the grainy pages of a Trotskyist broadsheet with nervously moist fingers. I loved the danger of extremist politics as a teenager and those same fingers, I have to admit, sometimes left marks on the corners of some right-wing magazines too – for sale at a different vendor, of course. Outside the cage I could look in, much as a gentle old maid might check out racy murder mysteries from her local lending library, the tigers if not paper at least safely under control.

## Pickering Arms

*In the year 920 King Edward the Elder founded a city here and called it Thelwall.* So says the 'olde worlde' sign on the external wall of the village pub, the Pickering Arms. On the inside walls in the 1970s hung polished brasses and cheap framed prints; over the bar, above rows of suspended wine glasses, some decorative plates sunk into lines of dust on a rack; and against the bar you would stand on orange swirls of carpet caked with ash and beer drippings. A place of intoxication and bloating (many would drink twelve pints of beer a session) where men legged it from dishwashing wives to return legless to the same wives, lonely in front of the telly or already in bed having an early night.

I had a job at this pub one summer, behind the bar . . . until I was sacked. First of all I couldn't add up in the heat and pressure of the moment and would use the cash register as my calculator, freezing its operation for the other bar staff. The landlord would arrive at the till, sweating and swearing: 'What the bloody 'ell . . .' As the place filled up with bodies and smoke, the thirsty punters became impatient punters. Pushing up to the bar, fat paws clutching cash, shouting their pints and gin and tonics and Cherry Bs into my ear. Beer was dispensed from a lozenge-like button with glasses held at an angle to minimise the froth. There were two cardboard boxes of white wine in the storeroom at the back, one sweet, one dry: 'If they ask for medium give 'em a shot of each.' The spirit measures pushed up to dispense from bottles hanging in front of a golden mirror, medicinal quantities, no room for a bartender's lax wrist or for the obscuring of the ice cubes' wall of shame. A fifth of a gill, and a bottle of sugary fizz dumped in. Tonic, ginger ale, lemonade, bitter lemon, coke – only the soberest palate could discern the difference as the evening drained away. 'Is that dead?' The used glass, base of spit and suds, lipstick prints on the rim, clinked away to the whirling brushes under the bar, hot to the hand, ready for a new mouth's thirsty slurp.

Was it the Cherry Bs? I knocked over a whole row of these ghastly liqueurs. Nothing broke but the bottles rolled about on the floor as if at a bowling alley. 'Jesus wept!' exclaimed the landlord in his favourite and oft-used curse. The shortest verse in the Bible. 'Be careful for God's sake. Christ!' Then under an impatient breath: 'Bloody useless . . .'

Then, one day, the coins. I handed them to a customer from my palm. 'Be right with you, sir,' I shouted to a different customer demanding a Guinness and blackcurrant. My hand was at the wrong angle, fingers stretched out but wrist pointing down. The coins poured into the beer's virgin froth. And I was out of a job.

## Harry's infallible left hand

It was Nicholas Ashton – yes, he danced the cancan to Harry Jarman's vamping at the Little Manor pub in Thelwall, near to the Pickering Arms where I had had my brief career as barman. Although vamp is not quite the right word. This pub pianist had an astonishing virtuoso left-hand technique, striding to the showtunes, Broadway reincarnated in Blackpool, with a jangle of slot machines alongside the rasp of fish and chips wrapped in newspaper. Harry Jarman. A homosexual.

Yes, he was described to me as that before I knew he was a pianist. He was well known in the Warrington area from his dance-band years but I was afraid to meet him and it seemed my mother encouraged that fear . . . for my safety? I adored Harry when we finally met, his camp demeanour, his gentle humour, his spectacular piano playing. Ask the pianist Ronan O'Hora about Harry Jarman and he will mention this leaping left hand, and his use of the second inversion 6/4 chord. It flew side to side without missing a beat, or a note. And without the lengthening ash from his drooping cigarette ever falling down on to his sharply creased grey trousers. A half pint of mild (a ladies' drink, in brew and volume) would wobble precariously on top of the upright piano – or was it a gin and lime? Fly me to the moon? No need. We were already there.

He did have one classical piece in his repertoire: Chopin's Second Scherzo, or at least its first page. The opening roll of triplets sounded like a petulant Pekingese: Dah, grrruff grrruff! Rhythmless and breathless. Or perhaps it was like the landlady dusting the piano keys the morning after a rough night in the pub, hairnet over her curlers, beer glasses piled high in the sink.

Later, when my mother had lost her sense of any danger, or I merely grew older, Harry used to come on occasion to our house in York Drive. With a friend. It was all so terribly innocent and I realise now how deep in the closet he was. I tried to raise the 'subject', but no. Gay men of that age (he must have been born in the 1920s) developed a reflex. Say too much and you might lose a tooth or a job, or even find the key turning in the prison door. Keep it bottled up, head down, hands on the keys of the old joanna. The love that dare not speak for shame. 'Another glass of mild, Harry?' 'Oh, I don't mind if I do, love.'

## Hazel

I first met Harry Jarman through Hazel Goynes – Quaker, pacifist, socialist and one of my favourite people. She was a naturally elegant woman, kind and tremendous fun. We'd hang out at her house and I remember the delightful craft work hung on her walls, her own stencilled or beaded pieces, collages, echoes of Paul Klee around her cosy rooms.

I need make no effort now to see once more Hazel's energetic gestures, her toss of the head as if by loosening her neck she might loosen her spirit. She had an uncompromising sense of fairness, and if perhaps her politics was sometimes expressed with naivety it was never smug or self-righteous. She was in her nineties when she died, unfailingly generous and warm, always a little ghost of Yorkshire in her speech.

We met when she was organising some kind of youth concert after I was in the finals of the BBC Young Musician competition. She came to our house one evening to discuss details and we all liked her instantly. Later, she became an even closer friend to my father and I think it was largely through her that my father somehow 'opened up' – a strange, powerful, midlife liberation leading him to the Open University (he got an excellent degree) and the open legs of numerous women – a success as notable, perhaps, as his late-in-life Humanities BA.

'I never had an affair with Colin,' Hazel once said to me years later, her eyes suddenly thoughtful and distant and a little tender. 'Hazel Goynes is not *im*-moral, she's *a*-moral,' said Auntie Liz bitterly, when she heard of my father's constant visits to Hazel's house. But then, if my mother was right, Liz was in love with my father. And then again, as I've said, she used on occasion to share a bed with my mother.

I knew nothing of all of this confusion at the time and was perfectly happy as long as the mugs of coffee were warm and the chocolate biscuits replenished.

## Dad the hippie

By the time I was at the RNCM Dad was definitely going through a hippie phase. No drugs (as far as I was aware) but, for a time, no underwear either. Beads were worn and longer hair and (hey man) a certain looseness of attitude, with a girlfriend (or two) in between. Poems were published in the Open University magazine (signed Colinhough – an e. e. cummings-esque gesture), and there were summer camps of self-discovery as part of the OU's TAD292 course in which, according to their website, 'bizarre games and happenings formed a part of [this] experimental residential course for a group of students at Sussex University. They were encouraged to make prints of various parts of their bodies. Some made bare bottom prints, other dragged rubbish through the streets.' He was having a whale of a time and it must have seemed sheer Technicolor compared to the sponge cakes and prayer meetings at home. When my parents decided to separate, my mother and I moved out of the family home in York Drive and many others moved in; it became a sort of commune: bedrooms and babies, bras hanging to dry in the dripping bathroom, unwashed coffee mugs and sticky spoons in the kitchen sink. My dad and his most serious girlfriend met at those Open University courses, two middle-aged, frustrated people seeking education and stimulation and fornication in some sort of hazy combo. Who knows what menopausal impulses can ignite when there's a sense of running out of time and where an essay on D. H. Lawrence (my father was studying *The Rainbow*) may lead one from writing about a lake to diving into one head first with loins ungirt?

In my childhood my relationship with my father was always difficult, and then, when my parents split up, I felt I had to take sides. My mother seemed to me the wronged one, forced to leave the home, and as I left with her and we definitely had a closer connection the choice was made for me. And there was no room for me in the commune. I'm sure my father's awkwardness with me had the deepest roots.

I found one of my grandmother's visiting cards in his papers: 'Mrs H. A. Hough and Colin'. I don't know of a shorter way to say both that he was the apple of his mother's eye and that he was hopelessly smothered.

Looking back I see I gave him no chance to be a warm, affectionate father. I just couldn't let go and open my hand or heart. I felt there was a barrier and I was routinely unkind in the things I said to him over the years. I don't think I ever really praised him. Things he wanted to talk to me about I'd make fun of. Since his death (aged fifty-five) not a month has gone past when I have not wanted to ask him something or share something with him. And whenever the late morning clock displays 11:11 I consciously think of him as I'm reminded each time of his birthday.

He was unexpected, brilliant, unfulfilled, imaginative, infuriating, interested and interesting in everything. A political maverick – strong views but allergic to dogmas or parties – he voted Liberal but was passionately opposed to Britain joining the EEC for non-conservative reasons. He ended up spoiling his ballot paper because he submitted an essay at the ballot box explaining why he was voting no. I wish he'd kept a copy. He had a nostalgia for the Empire (he was born in British Australia and lived his early years in British India) but he was resolutely left-wing and hated all prejudice and racism. He had had no musical training at all, but as soon as I started to learn the piano he became voraciously interested in classical music. He bought the steady stream of LPs which were my own education and amassed an extraordinarily sophisticated knowledge. From Monteverdi to Stockhausen he devoured music, and not just a straight path. He loved to veer off to side roads of folk and jazz and rock. Music moved him and he was unconcerned from where or how. He was often whistling: Boccherini, Bacharach, Bruckner . . . although Stockhausen did escape the purse of his lips, despite his having bought the LP of *Stimmung*. His total absence of musical education combined with boundless enthusiasm seemed to prevent pretension. It was too late to be told what kind of music one was meant to like; he'd already fallen in love. He hated snobbery in every form because it seemed to him (and he passed this along to me) fundamentally unintelligent.

His Open University degree was, I now realise, of huge importance to him. He was eighteen when the war ended and was forbidden by his mother to go to university. After a couple of extra years in the army in the Middle East he returned home to a country deep in the depression of post-war austerity. Money had to be earned, and without financial or social privilege or family support it was virtually impossible to pick up the pieces. Yet he did. As best he could. And I wish now I'd gone over to help wash those coffee mugs.

## Norman Baker

When I passed my eleven-plus the path was clear for me to attend Lymm Grammar School. But I was insistent: I wanted to go to a music specialist school. So when I was accepted at

Chetham's, and Cheshire County Council offered me some financial support, there was nothing to stop my going there. 'For all that has been, thanks; for all that shall be, yes' – Dag Hammarskjöld's pithy aphorism, enabling us to survey life front and back with healthy realism. In that spirit I'm grateful for the good and the bad in my years at Chets.

But one deprivation from not going to Lymm Grammar was missing out on studies with the music master there, Norman Baker. He became a dear friend when I was at college and beyond, and was indirectly responsible for one of my first transcriptions – *The March of the Siamese Children*, inspired by his school production of *The King and I* one Christmas. Each year a different show would be superbly, thrillingly performed by the students, produced by Norman and the art teacher Myra Worsley, who became another of my favourite Lymmites.

Norman played the organ at my reception into the Catholic Church in September 1980, and he played the organ at my mother's funeral thirty-six years (and three months) later. But when did we actually meet? I think it was probably Hazel, the great connector, who brought us together. But we became close (one never became *that* close to Norman – a hug was for him a trauma requiring an hour on the sofa with some smelling salts) as I continued my studies at the RNCM. Never was there a more warm-hearted man, or a more delightfully eccentric companion for a pub lunch. He cycled everywhere, spinning for miles along the Cheshire country lanes, his bald head shining in the sun between the clouds. He never appeared to eat very much; I think he saved his calories for pints of fine bitter at his favourite pub: 'They don't have any dreadful music there, and none of this food nonsense.'

We went down to London together in 1982 to choose and buy my first Steinway B. On the train we were much amused by the old-fashioned phrases peppering a series of letters he'd received from the Steinway salesman, a Mr Allen: 'On the 16th instant' – 'I beg to inform you' – 'your humble and obedient servant'. 'He sounds like a splendid fellow,' said Norman, relishing such archaic whimsy. He loved all manner of British quirks and eccentricities. It could be something like the churchwarden's obsession with prunes, or someone in the village with an excessive number of garden gnomes placed amidst her tulips . . . or a friend's puppet operas. I never actually witnessed one of Arthur Midgley's productions but we went to visit him once and I was astounded at the set-up. That year the opera was to be *Aida* and already, six months before, the preparations were well underway. The most intricate imaginable devices, strings and weights protruding and threading behind the wooden frame, computerised lighting and moving front curtain, a sinking stage on three levels, and the hand-painted 'singers': everything done with the utmost care. It was magnificent and mad, and all in a bungalow that seated perhaps a dozen people at a time.

Norman was very traditional and deeply conservative in so many ways, and when in his company you imagined the

British Empire might still be expanding (wider still, and wider), though more with prunes, gnomes and puppets than by conquering lands with bloodshed. We didn't share a love for Mrs Thatcher's handbag but we did share many hilarious times. Those parties at our house with Norman! The musical evenings at York Drive when he would play for me to sing Noël Coward, my hair slicked back, wearing a floor-length green silk dressing gown. Or we'd play duets with his friend Chris Arundale lying under the piano having emptied more than one wine bottle of its contents, smoking endless 'cigrettes', as he called them. Rhyming with 'regrets'. He had none (of the latter) and the ashtrays would pile high with Benson & Hedges Gold. He often showed up backstage at my early concerts in Manchester or surrounding towns and he'd present the gold box with a few fags peeking out. 'Benson's, Stephen?' And in those years I'd say, 'Oh yes, thanks Chris!' The match would flare and laughter would light up the dressing room.

## Tinkle of glass

By my final year at the Royal Northern I really felt settled. I'd worked hard and was enjoying my studies, and the memories of my destructive years at Chets were fading and irrelevant. I entered and won the college concerto competition playing Brahms's Second – in the same hall where I should have played it four years earlier in the BBC Young Musician competition, had I not run away scared. I remember a shocking moment in the audition, in the slow third movement. At the point when the music is at its most hushed and contemplative a light bulb exploded right above the piano with a bang, like a rifle shot. Of course, everyone in the concert hall jumped, including the pianist. A few seconds after the explosion I could hear a slight tinkle as bits of glass from the bulb fell from the high ceiling into the strings of the instrument.

The reward for winning the competition was to play this concerto with the college orchestra. I still remember the joy I felt in the second movement, surrounded by the vibration on stage of so many musicians playing their hearts out in that marvellous Brahms orchestration. Then along came the slow movement. All was fine until that moment when the music is at its most hushed and contemplative before . . . a light bulb exploded above the piano and I could hear a slight tinkle as bits of glass fell from the high ceiling into the strings of the instrument. For about a minute I was seriously spooked. This seemed beyond a coincidence. We finished the movement, with its slow, ascending B flat arpeggio replying to the solo cello's descent under the piano's trill, an exchange of utter intimacy and repose, and then came the fourth movement, sidling in on the subdominant, so exultant, yet so 'down to earth'. I've never felt, like some people, that this movement is a let-down after the rest of the concerto. For me it has always been an example of Brahms's perfect compositional judgement, and a moment of relief. After all, a light bulb can only explode once . . . or twice.

## All aboard to Juilliard via Pimlico

My trip to Euston for the National Junior Piano Playing Competition back in 1969 was my first London visit, and the same journey in 1980 for Philip Fowke's thirtieth birthday party was possibly only my third. I was now wearing long trousers, unlike that first visit, but I was still young, inexperienced and totally untravelled. Gordon Green, also Philip's teacher, had put the two of us in contact. I think the plan was for us to play some duets at the party but that never happened. I bought a new Samsonite suitcase for the occasion, but not one with wheels. How on earth I lugged it from the station to the Tube to Philip's flat in Pimlico I have no idea. I also brought along a pineapple as a gift for him, thinking it exotic and rare – I'd never seen one in Warrington except as slices or cubes in a tin. I was quite astonished to see that when Philip took a sharp knife to it later on there was not a round hole in the middle. And that it tasted so much better than the variety we had on Sunday evenings with evaporated milk after *Songs of Praise*.

Philip's house, his pianos (one of them had belonged to Benno Moiseiwitsch), his scores, his telephones, his desk littered with concert contracts, the bills, the letters – a life full of a professional musician's business and busyness . . . I was dizzy and disorientated. He'd invited me to stay overnight (hence the Samsonite) as the party would end late. People started arriving ('Hello darling!') and soon the rooms were filled with musicians, holding glasses of wine with ease, chatting, gossiping, laughing, confident, opinionated. I remember three people in particular. Firstly Bryce Morrison and his partner, Lyndon Scarfe. They became great friends of mine later on but all I recall from that occasion is Lyndon's splendid tie, knitted, thin as tissue paper, purplish.

Then there was Paul Bryanston. I stood open-mouthed with admiration at his sophistication and witty conversation, one assured idea after another, seemingly not a moment of doubt as words spilled from his wine-licked lips. The subject of teachers and America came up as I'd recently won the Royal Philharmonic Society's Julius Isserlis Scholarship and was deciding where to use it for study. Gathering up my courage, and finding a gap between the bon mots: 'So Paul, who are the best piano teachers in the United States?' Wine quickly swallowed and with a flourish of the hand, he cried: 'The *only* teacher to go to is Martin Canin at the Juilliard School.' End of sentence, end of story. So my decision was made, and within thirty seconds of hearing an unknown name, my future was settled. I didn't realise then that a confident opinion was not always a true one, and no one would have been surer of that than Paul himself. He was astonished in later years when I told him of his part in the jigsaw of my life – and even slightly horrified. But, in a strange way, I'm eternally grateful to him.

# JUILLIARD

# Across the Atlantic

'Room 303.'

She handed me the tarnished key on a thick, oblong plastic fob, larger than any pocket could accommodate or resident steal. It didn't come with a smile.

'Which way are the lif— the elevators?'

She looked up impatiently from the ledger she was studying and pointed with a blood-red fingernail.

'Over there.'

I smiled. 'Thank you so much.'

It would take me a year to adjust to, then to grow to love the rudeness of New Yorkers. The implication of ownership, of pride, of ease in their metropolis is intimidating to most newcomers. It helps to remember that Manhattan, though legendarily prominent, is actually small enough to get to know like one's morning face in the mirror. Some cities welcome guests eagerly, anxious to make the best impression. Others shun or distance themselves. New York, with a weary shrug, simply doesn't care. By now I've loved it and lived in it for over forty years.

On my first ever trip there, for my audition at the Juilliard School, I was staying at the Empire Hotel, directly across from Lincoln Center. At that time it was run-down and edgy, as was the city itself. I noticed as I entered my room that the door was made of solid metal, though shaped and painted as if wood, and for the first time since landing that first time at JFK airport I was reminded that New York was one of the most dangerous cities in the world in 1981. It had not yet recovered from the onslaught of 1970s unrest: drugs, racial conflict, gangs, pimps; dog eat dog in a town without kennels. But then the metal door was a comfort. No one would be able to shoot through that.

My audition was the next afternoon but I was too excited to rest, too curious. Apart from that trip on holiday with Margaret and Philip to Düsseldorf and a visit to Belfast I'd never flown before. After a brief flirtation with the idea of studying in Paris I'd decided on America. Perlemuter or Broadway? Having travelled so little, the double burden of making friends and learning how to communicate with them was too much. My O-level French would not have been a great start, and for someone who had lived so many years in a purple bedroom of dreams and fears America and English was enough to cope with. And it turned out to be more than enough, not least because the pound was worth around two dollars in those years, making my scholarship fund just about workable.

I walked about a bit but felt lost, despite the fact that it's almost impossible to lose your way on Manhattan's uptown grid. A walk up Broadway or is it Amsterdam Avenue or is it Columbus Avenue? The intersection is confusing until you know the landmarks. Apartments right there on the street, in the teeth of the town, at the spitting centre of everything. Groceries to door to restaurant to concert to bookshop to

dry-cleaners to bank to pharmacy, with one shopping bag.
The whole city a magnified bedsit/work/live/die pod. People
talk of Manhattan as the centre of the world; as I stood on
Broadway that first day it seemed self-evident.

## Bill's blue-eyed confidence

'Is this the right place to wait for the piano auditions?' I
asked the handsome guy with the black hair and blue eyes,
my question posed with 25 per cent ignorance and 75 per
cent concupiscence.

'Yeah. I guess we just wait here until they call us. I'm number fifteen. What about you?'

'I'm sixteen. Don't play too well!'

'Haha! This is my third audition in the past few weeks.
Trying for Peabody and Eastman too. I think I should have
a choice between the three and then I can decide. Rochester
sucks but it's a good school and the academics are better than
here at the Yard. But, you know. Juilliard. The magic name.
And New York is great.'

I'd only arrived in the *country* a few days before – on 26
February 1981. It all seemed so vast and new and over-
whelming. And the self-possession of this young student just
amazed me.

'What's your name? I'm Bill.'

'I'm Stephen. Hough. From England.'

'Oh cool. Which part?'

'Cheshire. I studied in Manchester.'

'Oh. I've been to London a few times. Terrible food but the museums are great.'

I'd never been to the museums in London myself, and I felt that inferiority complex which so many from the north have, leading them to over-compensate: *Oh, you like London, do you? I find it too loud and too many people.* But that wasn't my way. I slid under my Mancunian stone and blushed. He was probably going to win the audition over me anyway.

'What are you playing?' I asked, to change the subject.

'Bach Chrom. Fan., Hammerklavier, Fourth Ballade, Carter Sonata. What about you?'

His confidence seemed as big as his repertoire and suddenly my programme felt small and cautious.

'Bach A minor Prelude and Fugue Book Two, Beethoven opus 109, Franck *Prelude, Chorale and Fugue*, Messiaen, one of the *Vingts Regards*', the latter left deliberately vague so I could leave out the fact that I was playing the easiest one with the awkward French pronunciation. I was feeling more and more like a country bumpkin.

'Boy. No one plays the Franck any more,' he said, as if he knew exactly why, and it was not flattering to the piece or to my choice of it. 'I like it though,' he added, as if he'd seen my embarrassment but also as if he considered his positive opinion of it as raising its stock.

'The Hammerklavier?' I said. 'That's difficult in an audition situation. Maybe they'll ask for the fugue!'

'Oh, I hope they do. That's kinda my party piece. Been playing it since I was twelve.'

'Gosh, that's impressive!'

'Nah, not really. If you got the chops and the memory it's not so bad. And good trills. Trills have never been a problem for me. You just need a loose wrist.' He mimicked a trill on the side of one of the chairs where we were sitting and I was totally seduced by his all-American assurance. I wished he would have been mimicking the trill on my arm or knee.

'Who are you hoping to study with?'

'Josef Raieff, actually. I've had some lessons with him privately and he really likes my playing. He'll give me lots of freedom. I don't need a driller like Marcus at this stage. What about you?'

'Martin Canin.'

'Good guy.' Was he? Bill probably knew more about him than I did.

The young wiry secretary stepped out of the studio as we were speaking, and, as the previous pianist was leaving, she called Bill's name. He stood up with a spring and a cat's cradle crack of his fingers:

'Well, nice to talk to you, Stephen. Good luck with the audition. See ya around.'

I was sure now that I was not in the same league as these people and so I actually began to relax. Here I was in the famous Juilliard School. I wasn't going to be accepted so why should I care? I'd just play and enjoy the experience, and my mum would have videotaped the episodes of *Coronation Street* I'd missed. I'd watch them when I got home, leaning on the Aga with a bacon sandwich with HP Sauce.

About twenty minutes later Bill stepped out of the studio along with the wiry secretary. 'Stefan How,' she said. Well, how would she know? 'Steven Huff, actually,' I said, hesitantly, with a smile. She looked down at the sheet of paper, puzzled.

'Oh, I see. Well, it's your turn now.' Her humourlessness made me relax even more. It all seemed so surreal and silly. I'd asked for Martin Canin as my teacher, thanks to Paul Bryanston's recommendation at Philip's birthday party, but had not yet met him. I looked at the row of elderly teachers sitting at the back of the studio and saw the one that I knew was him from the photo – the youngest in the line-up. He looked friendly, as if he would be on my side. But he wasn't the one doing the talking.

'Can we hear the Bach Prelude?' said a strident voice belonging to a woman all folds and flesh and lipstick. I recognised the great Adele Marcus, with her reputation as a dragon, reducing students to tears with the ferocity of her fiery comments. I had a flicker of nerves again, but in a good way, serving to sharpen up my reflexes and make me concentrate and play with an edge. The Bach went well and after it the first movement of the Beethoven. Then she looked down at the table.

'What's this? Preemy . . . Airrr Communion dull a . . . Vi . . . Vierge. Hmmm. Could you play us the fugue from the Franck please?'

Marty Canin was smiling as I left and even Adele had a bemused curl of the lip, which suggested that disdain and contempt at least had been avoided. I was hoping to see Bill but he was nowhere to be found. So I went back to the Empire Hotel. It was over. Would I get in? Would I ever return to New York? Would Bill and I perhaps become roommates?

## Eline overlooking the river

We never became roommates (I have no idea where he went to study or where he is now), but I did pass the audition, and on 31 July 1981 my father and I landed at JFK and were met after baggage claim by Joan Simon, the friend of a (girl) friend of my father's who'd also met me when I arrived for my audition earlier in the year. On this second flight across the Atlantic I had two suitcases the size and weight of small propeller planes, one of them my grandmother's old wooden chest into which I'd packed all the scores and clothes I thought I'd need for the next two years. It ended up serving as a useful bedside table. Joan was a wonderful companion as we found our way around a city that was new to both us. My dad fell in love with New York as I had done. We walked all over the place, stopping to buy fresh orange juice on the street and drugstore lozenges to alleviate the pain from his stomach ulcers. Little did we know then that my father's annoying, constant pain was actually ravenous cancer devouring his insides day and night. He died about six months later aged fifty-five. We only started to get to know each other properly in New York, and then all was finished. Eaten alive.

But that was still the future. The present concern was to find somewhere for me to live before the semester began. We were astonished at how expensive New York was as we trawled from one Upper West Side building to the next in the sweltering August heat. Our base (temporary, thank God) was the Westside YMCA. I remember only a small room and a communal shower with roving eyes and the plughole a nest wriggling with pubic hairs.

But how on earth did I end up at the Imperial Court Hotel? Well, first we went to visit Eline McKnight, a friend of Philip Fowke's – he'd roomed with her when studying in New York with Rosalyn Tureck a decade earlier and had given me her details. I hoped that Eline would have space for me to live there. We soon realised that, without limitless funds, finding digs in New York was difficult. It was a world of under-the-table bribes and sleazy supers and furtive door-men. A success was to get the manager to lift his eyes up from the mini-television on the scratched desk to tell you that there were no vacancies. Everything was dishonest, lies upon lies.

Eline was not there when we arrived at the ornate doors of 100 Riverside Drive, but we waited a while and then she entered the lobby wearing large sunglasses and smoking a cigarette, with a straggly dog panting on the end of a leash. We introduced ourselves and liked her immediately as she took us up in the elevator to her apartment. As her front door opened, there ahead was a perfect view of the Hudson River from the living room window and, on the left of the room, a vintage Steinway B. The air was cool and it seemed like paradise after the endless slum trail we'd been on – those shoebox units with their rattling, dripping air-conditioning units, the dingy lobbies with their broken mailboxes reeking of roach spray. Eline's living room had a sofa bed along one side and no door, so it was not so private, but I was still anxious to move in. Except she already had a tenant.

She was an artist and had been part of New York's post-war art scene. De Kooning was a friend (there was one of his pieces hanging on the wall) and also the German painter Fritz Winter. She later gave me two of the latter's dark, expressionist paintings, on warped cardboard ('he had no money to buy canvas'). I thought they were rather ugly, with muddy textures, all browns and blacks and thick lines, but I framed them, kept them safe and still have them. She had a more impressive, attractive painting of Winter's on her wall, a bold work with a vivid red background. It was obviously one of her favourite possessions and, years later, she took it with her to the nursing home where she moved, but her brother sold it against her will. 'This place is bloody expensive. We have to get rid of all your valuables.' She was heartbroken. The irony was that he ended up in the same nursing home and actually died before her. A heart attack in the swimming pool.

I remember a few things about Eline. Her Dutch features complete with waves of blonde hair. The perspiration that would form on her upper lip in droplets. Her dog, Sumi, a ragbag of fur and bones who got her out of the apartment into the park. But then her depression. I don't know how clinical it was, and benefit of the doubt should always be the reflex response, but I feared asking her the routine 'How are you, Eline?' because I knew she would always say, 'Oh I'm so depressed.' There was no helpful response to this. If it was clinical then it needed professional treatment; if it was just a passing mood I felt inadequate to do more than try to cheer her up. And it seemed I usually failed. Nevertheless we became good friends and I spent many evenings at this apartment where I was never able to live.

Even though at this point Eline was in decline – divorced, weary, unmotivated, despondent – she still kept up her old tradition of occasionally holding musical soirées. There was a visitor's book in the hallway, started decades earlier, full of famous names from these gatherings. One evening I was there for a dinner party and after we'd all finished eating one of her friends sat down at the piano to play. The composer Lowell Liebermann, a fellow student and one of my best friends, was there too and he is to my funny bone what a lighted match is to a thin sheet of dry paper. This pianist began the sombre, melancholy melody of Szymanowski's B flat minor Etude. The serious-minded music lovers in the apartment were completely rapt and silent, determined to relish this experience as a taste of times past. But I made the mistake of glancing over at Lowell. He caught my eye and there was a twitch of his lips. I let out a snort of laughter which was impossible to disguise as anything else. No squeaky shoe or wriggle on the sofa could have faked it. I quickly started coughing as my cover-up and soon un-controllable giggles and stomach-wrenching coughs were combined in a cacophony and I staggered out of the room to Eline's bedroom, joining Sumi on the floor. My insides twisted in hysterical guffaws whilst the Szymanowski was subsiding from its central, passionate climax. It finished and there was enthusiastic applause. I sheepishly emerged from the bedroom, still hoping that my hacking facade had been a successful cover. 'I'm so sorry,' I said to the pianist who was wiping his brow. 'I had a terrible coughing attack.' His eyes were daggers and his lips curled in an expression of utter contempt. He knew. We never spoke again.

## Cockroaches and Proust

As Eline already had a lodger my father and I were back on the road, doorman to doorman, super to super, daily drawing blanks until we found (or I found – my father must have returned home by then) the Imperial Court Hotel on West 79th Street. The price was surprisingly low for a 'hotel'. Little did I know at that point what was in store for me there. It was the first place I lived which I could really call my own, so that made it special, but the room I rented was just dreadful. Not much bigger than the sagging double bed on which I slept, it was infested with cockroaches. There was a closet-kitchen with a hot plate which I could touch as I lay in bed, so cramped was the space; and in the diminutive bathroom there was barely room to move my arm from left to right to clean my teeth. My view from the grimy window was a crumbling brick wall and a rusting fire escape. But it turned out I was not living there alone. At nights, if I woke up, I would hear a gentle rustling. In my half-dreams I wondered: was it the trees of Riverside Park? Was it the waves of the Hudson River? No, it was a carpet of cockroaches on the floor, scurrying about. I discovered this one night when I switched on the light and saw a retreating army of vermin scuttle towards the safety of the kitchen area and disappear under the cupboard – three seconds flat and every one was gone, hushed, holding their breath before the light was extinguished again and they could reclaim the floor under my bed. And why not? After all, this planet has been their home for around 320 million years.

I remained at that apartment during that first, hot August. I bought insect spray and Roach Motels, small cardboard boxes with sticky insides to attract, then trap the little creatures: 'They check in, but they don't check out.' I would walk up West End Avenue to Eline's place and practise on her Steinway when her roommate was out, sipping chilled Tropicana orange juice, jealous of the serenity of that lovely, river-view apartment. Otherwise I just waited for my first Juilliard semester to begin. I knew no one in the city so I would sit in the window of my room as the darkness fell, next to the fire escape, and read from Volume One of the three large silver books I'd bought at Shakespeare & Co. on Broadway – the velvet beauty of Proust's prose some compensation for the ugliness of my surroundings.

But why didn't I explore the city more? Go out into the summer night of sin and sweat, across Manhattan's concrete lake, to sample the sensations on every numbered street or avenue? I don't know. I liked to hide away. Or maybe I hated it, but I hated more the fear of exposure, of opening my shirt buttons to the outside world. Left behind. The great childhood fear. The whoops of kids' games when we're not invited to take part. Better to pretend not to want to join in than wait, then fail to be asked. Outside the group. Out of fashion. Out of step. A cockroach hidden under the cooker.

The Imperial Court was gross but also disturbing. I mentioned to someone that I was living there: 'Oh heavens. That's an SRO hotel.' Somewhere they 'put' people. Not exactly locked away but . . . look away: the mentally ill, the destitute, the homeless. And then, one night. Someone had started a fire in their room. It was quickly extinguished but I opened my door to the smell of smoke and the sight of a woman running down the hallway screaming, dressed like a pink nun in flowing rose robes. School was about to start. It was time to move.

## Madame Borsuk

Madame Anna Borsuk was my landlady for the two years of my master's degree. It was a godsend of a living situation, better than Eline's apartment would have been in the end because I had my own private room and bathroom, and I was ten blocks closer to Juilliard. There was no piano there, but I think I am the person I am today because of that. I quickly started making close friends on the fourth floor of the Juilliard building and if I'd had a piano at home . . . well, perhaps I would have worked harder but I would have missed out on so many social encounters. If nothing else, I learned in my years at Juilliard how to overcome my earlier fear of friendship.

But how did I find Madame? I had a phone call from Joan Simon one day: 'Stephen, I've seen an ad for an apartment on West 71st Street, a spare room in a woman's apartment. She's looking for a "European" student. Shall I give you the details? It sounds promising.' I made the call and arrived at 235 West 71st Street, apartment 62, for my interview with my land-lady to be. 'Call me Madame' was not a Broadway show but rather her request as she held out a twig of a hand for me to kiss. She was an extraordinary-looking woman, all bones and rouge. A hunchback bird twisted into baggy clothes, lipstick as if applied with a paintbrush, reddened cheeks that would have made a doll blush, and her painted-on eyebrows an arch through which her beady eyes would peer.

The door to her room opened to the hallway and was always ajar, so I could not pass to my room without her see-ing me, unless she had dozed off. On the wall behind her chair hung a life-size portrait of her as Scheherazade. From a movie? She told me she'd had a career in silent films, and her exaggerated gestures and the wide-eyed way she'd ask if there was any milk left in the fridge did suggest such an earlier career. She even told me one morning that one of her movies had been on television the previous night – at 3 a.m., when only lonely actresses are still awake. I never saw one, or found out their names. Talking of TV, it was on in her room every time I returned home. It always seemed to be *Family Feud*. Did she have old episodes on video tapes? How could it possibly be playing so often? Richard Dawson's boredom was so evident in his banality; the spittle of the prettier women as he lip-kissed them was perhaps his only consolation in a mind-numbing show. And the fat cheque.

But Madame Borsuk was not an unintelligent or unrefined woman. She told me that she'd escaped from the Russian Revolution to Paris and then on to the United States. After a brief time in Hollywood she moved to New York and kept a Russian salon with her husband on 57th Street. 'Rachman-inov signed my piano.' 'Chaliapin was a regular guest.' But she sold everything after her husband died. It was as if her life was over. 'When he passed away I liquidated my apart-ment.' She's the only person I've heard use that word, with its additional suggestion of the past flowing away. So she sat, an un-merry widow, watching daytime TV until it turned to nighttime TV. The only difference was curtains drawn open or closed. It was sadder when they were open.

The whole apartment was dusty and faded, and much of it untouched. She sat in her little room at the back with a larger living room and two bedrooms unused, hence her interest in having a lodger. One time a group of us had had a late night and Lowell had missed his last train back to Long Island. He ended up staying at the apartment, sleeping in the spare bedroom on (top of) a single bed which had probably been last made up at least twenty years earlier. I don't think he removed his coat, never mind his clothes. I had no idea that Madame used that bedroom as a dressing room and, early in the morning, the door opened and she entered wearing only a billowing, unbuttoned nightdress. I heard a scream from her toothless mouth: 'Stefan, Stefan. There's a *man* in here.' All was easily explained, although I sensed a certain shiftiness in her manner after that. But she barely saw me as I would leave early and return late. She virtually begged me not to move when I announced, after winning the Naumburg, that I was signing a lease on my own apartment.

When I first began living there she would occasionally cook for me. I later declined the invitations when I saw the inside of the cupboards with roach droppings and the now-dead husks of the creatures that had left such a disgusting trail all over the pans and plates. Cutlery was rinsed under a cold tap and placed straight back in a drawer. Everything was caked with old food. There was a smell of decay in every corner. But an early meal provided me with an anecdote I've told many times over the years. It was the beef stroganoff. 'Madame, this is delicious! Do you think I might have the recipe?' 'Oh, I don't like to give it to anyone. You see, General Stroganoff wrote it out for me himself.' There aren't many better name-dropping stories. But by 1981 perhaps a few dead cockroaches had added something to the Russian sauce's flavour.

## Friends and the cafeteria

On the first morning of my new life at Juilliard I discovered that my graduate degree from the RNCM was academically not quite sufficient for me to begin a master's. Ear training would have to be done for another year as I was unfamiliar with the mandated rhythmic dictation system (a ridiculous, tongue-twisting waste of time), and I'd previously done no History of Western Culture studies. The ear-training classes were tedious but effortless, but the HWC course, with Beatrice Tauss, turned out to be fascinating.

Hunger on the first morning took me to the cafeteria on the second floor and I can't count the hours I ended up spending there. The food was abysmal – foul coffee from a rancid, rusty machine (students spoke of occasional cockroaches swimming in the dispensed beverages), and toasted sandwiches, their surfaces lubed up with oil so they'd slide on and off the griddle. I sat down wearing a thick Harris tweed jacket and a dorky tie, and smoking a pipe. Perhaps it didn't seem quite as eccentric back then (oh yes, it did!) but I couldn't imagine dressing any other way, and now I can't imagine what was on my mind. Everyone was smoking, but my aromatic cloud – my tobacco pouch, my tamper, my pipe cleaners – was fairly unusual.

It was in the cafeteria where we often forged friendships. I met Lowell Liebermann by chance there one day when I overheard an argument he was having with another student about Shostakovich. I edged over to listen, joined in a little and then, finding out he was a composer, asked whether he'd written anything for piano. Only his First Piano Sonata existed at that point but I requested a copy, learned it, and became its proud dedicatee a few months later. There were interesting, serious discussions but more often one heard statements like: 'Nah, I don't wanna record for CBS. Their piano sound is not great. I'll hold out for RCA.'

Dancers were the most visible students as they flexed limber limbs and pranced around in their leotards, showing off their developing bodies. We all fancied the dancers. I was too intimidated even to talk to them. Except one – was his name Jimmy? I got John Nauman to invite him round to his apartment for a drink one evening so we could meet. Amazingly he agreed, arrived and then sat, coiled elegantly on the sofa, waiting to be entertained or to find out why he was there. I'd cooked the one dish in my repertoire, spaghetti bolognese. 'Er, thanks, but I've already eaten.' A frightful, awkward ten minutes of half-conversation passed as the pasta got cold in John's kitchen. Eventually he stifled a yawn and glanced at his watch. 'Hey, I must go. See you around.' I never did.

In no special order . . . Lowell Liebermann, John Nauman, Neal Gripp, Donna Weng, Seann Alderking, Ezequiel Viñao, Stefan Lindgren, Pascal Nemirovski, Tony Byrne, Bob Neu, Bruce Wang, Jonathan Bass, David Frost, Erika Nickrenz, Tom Kaurich, David Nish, Francine Kay, Norman Krieger, Paul Verona, Sung-Kuk Kim . . . I can't say more about these friends from that time. Too many memories rise to the surface. Many of us spent every waking hour together. I see them all, as if before my eyes. Some I've loved. Some I've lost touch with. Some have now died. All are treasured as I think of them again.

Many came to visit me when I was in Lenox Hill Hospital for a week in my second year. It was 1982, the middle of the second semester, and something had been gnawing away at my energy and my stomach. I was utterly exhausted, unable to eat and creased through with pain, barely able to stand. I left my apartment one afternoon almost on my knees and took a taxi to the emergency room at Roosevelt Hospital on Ninth Avenue. 'Sexual orientation?' was almost the first thing I was asked as I slouched in pain in the nurse's office. AIDS was still being referred to as GRID at that point. As she ticked 'option two' when I answered her question, I flinched in fear. Would I live until graduation?

## Random teachers at Juilliard

Jacob Lateiner was a brilliant man, someone passionate about text and the importance of musical intelligence, but also someone often obsessed with text and blinkered by musical intelligence. I never had piano lessons with him (I wish in a way I had) but I took his Beethoven seminar and was stimulated week by week by his insights and revelations. He was on the jury of the Naumburg Competition I was later to win, and he approached me after the result had been announced: 'You played ze Haydn like an *angel* . . .' – born in Havana to Polish Jewish parents, he never lost that mid-European accent that spoke of fine coffee and choice cigars (he indulged in both with relish, keeping an espresso machine in his teaching studio) – 'but your Chopin was HORREN-DOUS!' I've had some back-handed compliments in my time but that one put wind into, then out of, my sails with matchless gusto, rare as one of the malt whiskies he also loved. ('Fifteen years is the perfect age. Older and the taste has gone, younger and it has not yet matured.') My 'horrendous' Chopin did nothing to stop him inviting me and Lowell Liebermann to his apartment for a taste of his Scotch collection one evening. We always said we'd get together for dinner. We never did.

David Diamond – another connection with Lowell, who was his composition student. Diamond managed to mention homosexuality in most classes and he usually wore an emerald-green tie. He was famous so everything he said contained a glint of gold for me. But the years have passed, the gold has worn away, and all I can remember is a wonderful evening at Fulton's bar on Broadway and 71st Street, at the end of the block where I lived with Madame Borsuk. We sat and chatted, about six of us. He drank a good number of Wild Turkeys. 'It's like a barnyard in here,' he said, with a characteristic puckering of his lips. Oh, and there was that occasion at his seventieth birthday concert at Merkin Hall when for some reason (I can't remember why) I actually arrived with him. We walked into the auditorium together and there was Leonard Bernstein sitting on an aisle seat with a cigarette holder in his mouth. Diamond introduced us (they'd been friends and possibly more for years) and Lenny looked me up and down without a smile or a word. I noticed an elderly lady in sunglasses sitting next to him – I glanced at her without much of a thought. It turned out it was Greta Garbo. Now *her* I would have liked to have been snubbed by!

Irving Kolodin – this doyen of American music critics taught a seminar on music criticism. His voice had a certain monotone which failed to bring his subject to life – perhaps he was just shy and reserved in front of students. We didn't realise that he was taping all his lectures until one day he literally stopped mid-sentence (did he hold his breath too?), opened the machine, flipped the cassette tape over, then continued. His detachment from both his students and his subject was demoralising. Teaching should be as creative as improvisation, and even if everything is planned, it should never sound like that. Archbishop Fulton Sheen wrote that he destroyed his lecture notes every year to maintain freshness.

Joseph Bloch taught piano literature. I really enjoyed his classes as we hurtled around the corners of the repertoire. He was always smiling and indulging his dry sense of humour – his jaw had a way of dropping down and nestling low as he laughed. I never spoke to him outside the class but he wrote me a reference which singlehandedly enabled me to enter the Naumburg Competition in 1983. So my life without Jim Bloch could have been very different.

William Masselos was dismissed by Adele Marcus as a teacher who didn't teach anyone anything, but he was probably the most cultured pianist on the faculty at the time. He had premiered Charles Ives's Piano Sonata no. 1 (forty years after it was written) and Aaron Copland's massive *Piano Fantasy* when the ink was still wet on the page. He was also an extremely kind man. After I won the Naumburg I learned Ben Weber's *Fantasia (Variations)* which was dedicated to him, and I phoned him one day to ask if I could play it for him. I went over to his apartment and as we talked I began to wish that I'd been studying with him for the entire two years of my time at Juilliard. He was already ill with Parkinson's and I remember the awful awkwardness as he tried, with difficulty and frustration, to put an LP onto the turntable. He wanted me to hear more of Weber's music as a reference.

Felix Galimir was assigned to me for chamber music studies, but I didn't realise at the time what a distinguished past he'd had – the Galimir Quartet had recorded Ravel and Berg in the 1930s with the composers present at the sessions. I worked with Tomoko Kato on violin sonatas, including the Brahms D minor. The awkward unison passage in the fourth movement was always too loud for him. 'It's tricky on this piano, Mr Galimir,' I said, by way of an excuse. 'I've heard it softer on that piano,' he replied with a smile.

Beatrice Tauss was perhaps the best teacher I had in my two years at Juilliard. Yes, a lovely irony that I had to travel all the way to a music conservatory in America to learn about English literature. A fellow student at the time, Sara Davis (then David) Buechner, wrote online after her death how 'her eyes positively glistened as she shared the wonders of Goethe and Dante and Shakespeare with us, making the classics vital, thrilling, and even, dare I say, sexy . . . Most of all I will remember those eyes aglow with radiance.' Me too.

## This just isn't your piece, dear

In my two years at Juilliard I had two different piano teachers – Martin Canin and Adele Marcus. I wrote earlier about why I chose to study with the former. The first piece we worked on in the first semester was the Schumann Fantasie op. 17 and although, as I played it week by week, Mr Canin had really good ideas, I began to be disturbed by how fixed they were. I'd been used to a wider landscape of possibilities, encouraged by my teachers in Manchester, a sense that interpretation was something as creative as the composer's music we were playing, a sense that *rubato* was something to be explored on the spot, not fixed on the page. Mr Canin would squiggle little *rubatos* in pencil on my score, with great precision, and then be surprised when, a week later, I was doing them in a slightly different place. This felt to me like a vice tightening on my musical growth, a shrinking and a domesticating of something that must run wild if it is to be alive. I realise now he was grooming my pieces to make me assured of winning competitions or passing auditions. It made me very uncomfortable.

I'd only planned to spend two years at Juilliard (that was the length of my Royal Philharmonic Society scholarship) and around the cafeteria tables the talk was all about other teachers: Nadia Reisenberg and her beautiful tone; Rudolf Firkušný, who took only a few students and whose studio was so difficult to get into; and Adele Marcus, the former assistant to Josef Lhévinne and the *grande dame* of the keyboard faculty. She was known for her outbursts of anger and her volatile temperament, also for her success in creating hyper-virtuoso techniques as a golden-age link to the past. As I wasn't keen to continue with Mr Canin I phoned Miss Marcus and asked if I could play for her with the possibility of switching to her studio for my second year. Today at Juilliard the culture of studios and teachers is totally different. Now it is encouraged to have a wider pool of influence in students' formation – I myself have shared each of my students there with other teachers. But in those possessive days even to look with anything but an evil eye at one of the other professors was to risk being ticked off at best. And for a student to change from one studio to another was an unforgivable sin.

When I called Mr Canin to tell him that I wanted to switch teachers it felt as if all the phone lines in Manhattan had suddenly frozen. We spoke for forty minutes as he tried to persuade me not to make the move. 'Come and see me tomorrow, Stephen, and we'll discuss this some more.' A night's sleep had obviously not made Mr Canin any mellower when I arrived next day at his studio, and I sensed anger as well as deep hurt in his manner towards me. We never had a proper reconciliation, although occasionally I would pass him on the street (we lived a few blocks from each other on

West End Avenue) and we would nod pleasantly in greeting. A colleague told me, years afterwards, that Martin was sorry we'd had that rift but that he'd really admired me as a student and felt betrayed by my lack of loyalty.

Looking back, forty years later, I regret our rift as he was a highly intelligent man and a fine musician. Actually I think he bore a deep-seated resentment at having been the long-time assistant to the overpowering personality of Rosina Lhévinne. You can see him in some video footage of her classes, young, handsome, but little more than an accompanist or secretary figure in the background – and in a class of dazzlingly successful contemporaries.

Moreover, as my lessons with Adele Marcus continued I actually wondered if I'd made a mistake by making the change. In place of the pencil squiggles on the score were huge scrawls in blue ballpoint pen: fingerings bigger than the notes, circles around things, random comments. My favourite was 'Somewhat too'. She'd failed to include the adjective, but there it was. An indelible mark of dissatisfaction. One fellow student's score of the Liszt First Concerto was almost an artwork. Adele had placed her pen on the paper, drawn a spiral over the whole page and then, from top to bottom, ripped the metal tip down, tearing through at least one sheet. Another student recalled playing the Second Scherzo of Chopin for her. At the end Adele went over to the piano in annoyance: 'The first chord is all wrong, dear.' And she proceeded to play the opening of the *First* Scherzo.

By this point in her life (she was already in her late

seventies) there was a chaos, a frustration and an illogic in her mind that were very disturbing. One morning I brought her Beethoven's last sonata, op. 111. Rather unusually she asked me to start with the second movement, the slow, serene variations in seamless C major. I began, and within three seconds she interrupted, 'Dear, it's too slow.' I moved the pace along a bit: 'It's too loud, it's not quite . . .' I stopped and looked at her. 'This just isn't your piece, dear. Learn the Schubert D major instead and bring the first movement to me next week.' So I left, having played about eight bars, and went off to buy the score of the Schubert. A few days later the phone rang: 'Dear, it's Adele Marcus here. How are you? Now I'm giving a class soon in Chicago and I'd like you to come along with me and play. Will you bring the Beethoven op. 111?' 'But Miss Marcus, you told me it wasn't my piece and to learn the Schubert D major instead.' 'Nonsense, dear. You played it gorgeously.' What? All eight bars?

Perhaps my favourite lesson was when I took the John Ireland concerto to her. I had four performances to play with the Hallé Orchestra and James Loughran on a UK tour, including my Royal Festival Hall debut. She'd never heard of John Ireland and certainly never heard this piece but she seemed enchanted as, with Danny Lessner on second piano (he's the pianist playing *Rhapsody in Blue* on United Airlines as your plane is taxiing to the runway), we ran through this homespun English period piece. We got to the jaunty second subject of the first movement and she started dancing next to the piano with her hands in the air: 'Dear, I just *love* this music! It's so *Jewish*.' I could only imagine the composer's be-musement being even greater than mine at that moment, the Anglican organist from Bowdon entertaining the thirteenth child of an Orthodox rabbi from Kansas.

Any account of Adele Marcus cannot leave out her tem-pestuous moods and her often destructive comments. But no account of her should fail to convey her warmheartedness. She did care about her students, even if in an overbearing, jealous, competitive way. At my first lesson with her, at her apartment, she asked if I'd like some vodka in the orange juice she brought me. I declined but still stayed there for over three hours. On another occasion I did accept her offer of some vintage brandy and so much was consumed that she was unable to get up to answer the door: 'One drink, one drunk,' she slurred as I went to let in my friend Stefan Lind-gren, who was meant to be having a lesson. And after Stefan had had some brandy himself and left, she took me out for dinner. We were together that day for over five hours.

I remember once going with her to a restaurant on Am-sterdam Avenue called Sweetwaters. It was a sort of high-class diner and we had delicious steaks. At the end of the meal, looking over her reading glasses at the menu, she said to me: 'Now dear, I never touch desserts but *you* must have one. They say the chocolate turtle pie is especially delicious.' We summoned the waiter over. He smiled at her: 'So, Miss Mar-cus. Will you be having your usual, the chocolate turtle pie?' Her wink and smile to me at being caught out was a lovable indication of her fun, and of her generosity.

She was a complicated person (aren't we all!), but despite everything (another year with her and I doubt I would have had any confidence left) I still treasure her memory. And I learned some things from her, amidst the madness, which inform everything I do at the piano to this day.

## Attending concerts in New York

It always amazes me how few students seem interested in attending concerts, even when they require only a five-minute walk to occupy a free seat. Shouldn't the privilege of studying at college be incentive enough to take every opportunity to hear live performances?

Er, yes. I do believe that, but I think in my two years at Juilliard I went to fewer than a dozen concerts outside the building. I saw some operas – *Parsifal* twice in one week, a lot of standing; but I was at bars more than once every week – also a lot of standing. Higher education is a time to be educated of course, but the rebellion of putting aside studies for some fun can be an important stage of personal growth. I developed more as a musician through my friendships than I might have done sitting in front of the piano for ten hours a day. I did, however, attend some concerts. Some great ones.

Vladimir Horowitz was the first, at the Metropolitan Opera, and the anticipation of hearing on stage a legend I'd loved for years on recordings was enormously exciting. Interestingly, Earl Wild was playing the very same afternoon, 1 November 1981, at Carnegie Hall, a programme consisting entirely of transcriptions, which, like Horowitz's concert, was eventually released commercially. One of Wild's students, when I asked him which concert he would be attending, said, 'Oh, the one by the better pianist.' I asked my teacher, Martin Canin, which one he would attend: 'Neither. I'm going to stay at home.'

I regretted not being at Earl's recital but he didn't really seem legendary to me at the time, and I imagined I'd be able to hear him again on many other occasions. Such a programme as Wild's in the early 1980s was still considered shocking and it would be an audacious choice even today, but Horowitz was Horowitz. His Met recital turned out not to be his greatest playing but the charisma of the man and the 'force' of his *pianissimos* was utterly compelling. There was a moment in that vast auditorium (I was sitting near the back in a cheap seat) when my heart stopped. He took sound to the edge of the edge. It wasn't just playing softly – there was a *presence* to the sound, his timing capturing the phrase, his arm weight sinking the key gently down to the point of caress. Like a snooker player, Horowitz knew how to pocket a ball so that it fell into gravity's arms, seeming merely to brush the netting of the aperture as it descended.

Dame Moura Lympany was the greatest surprise. A week after Horowitz's recital a friend came up to me in the cafeteria: 'I've got some free tickets for this British pianist, Moura Lympany. D'you wanna come?' 'Oh, I don't think so. She's no good,' I replied, the bumptious student knowing her only from the budget Grieg and Schumann concerto LP

I'd had as a child and which I'd barely listened to in a decade, and sensing from her more the buzz of society lunches, with flighty gowns, and hair by Rodney, than a serious pianist:

'Oh darling. You've never looked lovelier or more glam. Playing at Carnegie Hall are we? You know what they say, don't you: how do I get to Carneg . . .' 'Yes, yes, Rodney. I know that joke. Now run along. My dressmaker is coming in half an hour and I simply must get home.' 'Of course, my love . . . Bitch!', he said under his breath. 'I should have given you a beehive – if you had enough hair to create one. Mere wisps . . .' His sibilant 'S's whistled through the air but Moura heard nothing as she bustled her way to the exit. 'My secretary will arrange payment, Rodders. Bye, darling.' She flounced out into the Mayfair street with a confident smile, looking around for possible admirers.

It just didn't seem that Dame Moura would be great, but how wrong I was! The Haydn E minor Sonata that opened was charming, with a kind of old-fashioned delicacy that enchanted. Schumann's *Etudes Symphoniques* was also very fine. But then, the second half. I don't remember everything but Debussy's 'Reflets dans l'eau', Ravel's 'Ondine' and Liszt's 'Feux Follets' were simply staggering. Such a sound and such gossamer textures. It was a triumph, she was showered with flowers from adoring fans, and I was happy to have been proved totally wrong.

Christian Blackshaw also played in New York that month, the Britten Piano Concerto and *Young Apollo* with the New York Philharmonic and Raymond Leppard. Christian was Gordon Green's favourite pupil and I think all his younger students looked up to Christian with a kind of reverence. I first heard him at the Royal Exchange Theatre in Manchester giving a lunchtime recital including the Bartók Sonata. It was a fabulous concert, hugely impressive, assured, polished, with total conviction and acute sensitivity. I felt proud that I was part of the same stable as him, especially sitting in 1981 in Avery Fisher Hall, so far from our Cheshire homes. Then the Britten Concerto began. Great, clean, clear, incisive playing. I've never heard it better. But I was suddenly overcome by a sort of creeping embarrassment about the music itself, a physical flinch of dis-ease. We were in the heart of buzzing New York, at Lincoln Center, and then this . . . this English *thing*. This summer fete of a piece. This village green of a piece. Britten made me ashamed of being English. It was like being forced indoors into a hot sitting room for stale afternoon tea and polite conversation when outside there were mountains to be climbed and rivers to be crossed. I love Britten, more now than ever, but that day that piece sat in my stomach like a heavy scone.

I was nervous but I went backstage to say hello to Christian afterwards. 'What are you doing here, Stephen?' 'I've just begun studying at Juilliard.' His face fell with disapproval. 'Why would you want to study in New York?' he asked in a tone that demanded either an embarrassed 'I don't know. I wish I were back in Europe' or a vigorous defence for which my nineteen years had not yet prepared me. I mumbled something about having a great teacher and having a scholarship and gaining experience – and I left the backstage, out into Manhattan's crisp night. I mention this encounter because many emotions coalesced that evening in that hall. My leaving England and moving to America had felt, at that time, at that age, like a release from prison, a flinging open of windows; and Benjamin Britten seemed like an old uncle calling me to return to the Old World. I'd only been living in New York for three months and my perspective shifted later, but it was a perfect example of Dylan Thomas's description of the two nations 'up against the barrier of a common language'.

I've already spoken about Jacob Lateiner's amazing Beethoven seminar and his wonderful, stimulating company. But on stage, on the two occasions I heard him, he was not at his best. In passage after passage I sensed an unease, a nervousness and, at times, even blind panic. There was magnificence here and there, but it was frustrating because I sensed I was missing out on a potentially great performance as I sat there feeling deeply uncomfortable. He played Mozart's concertos K491 and K503 in one concert at the Metropolitan Museum, and on another occasion Beethoven's Emperor Concerto at the Cathedral of St John the Divine. I went backstage to see him after the Mozarts and he was obviously embarrassed: 'Excuse the little shits,' he said to me, blushing and turning away. He had impossibly high standards for his students and on stage he had found them difficult to live up to himself. Now he is no longer alive, all that nervousness a distant memory, but some superb recordings survive.

## Smoking and showing off on the fourth floor

Practising? Well, I spent a lot of time on the fourth floor at Juilliard, which was where the practice studios were – row after row of rooms with small Steinways and semi-soundproof doors, a vast cacophony of effort and improvement and stagnation and showing off, a classical music stew of fugues and cadenzas and octaves and scales and Scriabin and . . . cigarettes. Hard to believe now, but most students smoked in those practice rooms. Many of the arms of the pianos were scarred with a charcoal furrow where a cigarette had been balanced and left to burn down.

But the fourth floor was also a sort of club into which we checked every morning and often left only when the school closed – was it at ten o'clock at night? If I had practised constantly during my many hours there my repertoire would be endless, but it was talk which was endless, sitting down on the yellow-carpeted corridors or hanging out in each other's rooms. A room was yours if it was empty and you nabbed it, no booking involved; and like some car-parking slots, it could be kept by feeding the meter, in this case leaving a score on the music rack. You were given fifteen minutes' grace for a bathroom visit, a coffee fix or a phone call (this was before mobiles, of course), but if you were not back at the keyboard by then, it was free for someone else. The system seemed to work and only rarely were there arguments. Some people preferred one studio over another: this one at the end of the corridor with a mellow-toned piano for the serious worker, that one near the elevator with a screamingly loud piano (and bad sound insulation) for the pianist who wanted the whole world to hear her Chopin étude.

I remember one pianist whose Prokofiev Toccata was extraordinarily brilliant who would take one of the louder studios and show off his pile-driver technique. It sounded as if the room were being renovated rather than the piece practised . . . and it was thrilling. Then there was Michael Gurt standing outside my room one day as I was working on the *Caprice-Burlesque* of Gabrilowitsch. 'What's that?' he said as he entered, grinning and chewing gum – I never saw him not chewing gum. He asked to borrow the score and by the end of the afternoon he had perfected and memorised that virtuoso bonbon. It was truly impressive. There was Momoro Ono's spellbinding Liszt 'Feux Follets', one of the great performances in history, except he would never play it for anyone. You had to creep up to the room and catch the fireflies from outside, elusive wings disappearing in a gentle buzz.

Some pianists were always learning new repertoire; others, after two years, were still playing the same pieces. There were small windows in every room so one could walk around, watching and listening, admiring or criticising. I remember a Schumann Toccata endurance contest when both students began to play it super-fast to see whose arm gave up first. But in Adele Marcus's studio there was more a cult of sound. It wasn't who had the best octaves or double notes but whose tone glowed richer, whose *cantabile* carried the singing line most tellingly.

Sometimes a student would just barge in during a practice session. I was reading through the *Java Suite* of Godowsky once from dozens of loose Xerox pages when the door opened. 'What are you practising?' said the student as he walked over to the piano to look. He picked up the sheets, glanced through them, then dropped them confetti-like on the floor and left. Later we became great friends and later still he was very kind to me at a time of personal crisis. Others would offer advice, often useful, often obnoxious. I was chatting with one student on one occasion: 'Stephen, you could be one of the greatest pianists in the world . . .' He paused and I blushed. 'But not if you keep playing the way you are.' I blushed some more. Strange how the same blood in the same cheeks can mean two totally different things.

## Chita, Katie and Olegna

For a month or two in my first year in New York I earned some money playing the piano in a nightclub – the New Ballroom on West 28th Street. I visited this establishment over Christmas 1981 with Philip Fowke when we had Sunday brunch to the accompaniment of Gershwin himself playing. It was their gimmick: they had a Knabe player-piano with piano rolls of the great pianists of the past. They must have been looking for living pianists too, and somehow I got the job to play background music in the bar when Chita Rivera was taking a break from her show in the main room. I had a small repertoire of light popular music

– Billy Mayerl from my Winnie Monk days, along with some standards from the musicals of the 1950s. I also had a few subdued, soft-centred classical works which I could tinkle away at in the corner. I was a huge failure. I don't think I ever got any tips during my time there. The only reward I remember, apart from my small pay cheques, was a massage of my shoulders by one of the managers of the club at two o'clock in the morning as I was about to leave. My muscles instantly became tight in revulsion and I stood up quickly to get out of there. A phone call from him a day later relieved me of my duties as substitute for Mr Gershwin. It was a huge relief because my morning studies and a late-night job were an incompatible combination.

But I needed to find another way to earn some money. Katherine Parker taught piano in the Pre-College at Juilliard where she herself had studied with Rosina Lhévinne, and accompanying her students in their concertos, mainly on Saturdays, became my sole source of income apart from my scholarship money. I suppose it would have been more useful to be attached to the studio of a string or woodwind teacher as I could then have got some chamber repertoire under my belt, but instead my task was to play the (often extremely awkward) two-piano reductions of orchestral scores. My first assignment was Kabalevsky's Third, his 'Youth' Concerto. I arrived at her apartment on West 86th Street, took off my coat and struck up the breezy, bright D major intro. I never looked back. It was a regular job for two years and Miss Parker and I got along tremendously well. She was an elegant, unmarried lady from the South, always gracious despite the occasional barb aimed at one of her pupils: 'Don't play so loudly, dear. The neighbours will think it's me.'

I had a similar job with Olegna Fuschi who was director of the Juilliard Pre-College. She was like a glamorous movie star to Katie's Mother Superior. She had tremendous energy as, in addition to streams of students coming and going in her studio and a full-on administrative job, she also had a full concert diary. And a full life. I recently saw a photo online of her dancing a mazurka with Arthur Rubinstein. I can't quite imagine Katie with her arms around the Polish virtuoso.

## Eating in the early years in New York

I had my first sushi with my father during that first pre-Juilliard summer, at Dan Tempura on 69th Street and Broadway. I hated the raw fish then, but it was a taste of my new life in a new city in a new country on a new continent. I eat sushi now at least once a week.

Once the semester began, the American Restaurant was my regular haunt – also on Broadway, on the same side, but a block north. It was later renamed the Westside Restaurant and a group of us would go there after school most days. Burgers in Manchester and in my mother's kitchen had been the thickness (and flavour) of cardboard, but here in New York they were thick and tasted of steak. I'd usually have the Cheeseburger Deluxe, fries as thin and crispy as the burger was plump and juicy – although the orange, plasticky cheese slice melted on top could have used some improvement. Iced water, limitless coffee, baskets overflowing with bread – America's amnesia of austerity. Food was quickly ordered, quick-cooked in the sweatshop kitchen; plates quick-slid from hairy arms onto the Formica table top, invisible under the mounds of food, edging to the limit, everything piled, heaped, stacked, pressed together. 'A napkin please', and a wodge of paper would arrive, a phone book, *War and Peace*. Big skies; big stomachs; big hearts.

Pizza in Warrington had been yet more cardboard (did the contents taste much different from the packaging?), out of the freezer, frost on the neon-red tomato topping. But in New York large disc-pies were skimmed out from ovens on spatulas to be wheel-sliced into curling, flavoursome triangles, folded into a watering mouth. I'd learned to use chopsticks in Manchester with Ka Kit Tam, my friend and fellow student at the RNCM, and we did go occasionally to Chinatown restaurants; but at home it was only take-aways: chow mein, foo yung, or that sweet 'n' sour pork from Latchford. I cut one of the segments open once rather than chewing it whole and searched in vain for any meat amidst the white fat inside the fatty batter. New York had proper Chinese food from different regions, and Empire Szechuan became a favourite. I must have eaten there hundreds of times over the years, most memorably with Lowell Lieber-mann when it was the only show in town, 100th Street and Broadway, on the evening of 9/11 itself.

## Closets and bars

Arriving to live in New York City in 1981 as a gay man, although not an active or open one, was a recipe for potential disaster. AIDS was there in full force but completely unknown and invisible. Many people I knew from the 1980s are now dead and my own experience of Manhattan and homosexuality is a very poignant cocktail.

I knew I was gay before I knew what it was, and I described earlier in this book my first sexual experience with another boy, before I was five years old. I was still pretty much in the closet when I began at Juilliard but, like many university students, we can live in different closets in different cities. At home we might appear to be looking for a girlfriend or say we're too busy to find one, whereas at college everyone knows that it's really a boyfriend we want. The world is completely different today (I'm still astonished when a young person can talk openly about being gay), but in 1981 I felt that my homosexuality had to be hidden from most friends and relatives back home. Added to that, I was a recently converted Catholic and I was learning to live with the idea that I was required to be celibate for the rest of my life. Actually, New York had enough allure in itself to compensate for any lack of personal romance or titillation, despite the frequent crushes and the infrequent fooling around. I was loving being in the city, I was loving being at Juilliard, and, for the first time in my life, I had a wide circle of friends I saw regularly.

There was much gay talk in the Juilliard cafeteria, and

many friends, both gay and straight, would join in the chatter and come along to visit the bars. I never went alone to these places, always a tourist not a resident, and I'd stand in the corner nursing a bottle of beer, observing coyly, not planning to hook up or even speak to a stranger. New York's gay scene was extremely lively and a walk around Greenwich Village meant stumbling across dozens of gay establishments and hundreds of openly gay people – the full spectrum from flouncing drag to scowling leather. I went into most of the bars at that time, from the fairly innocuous Uncle Charlie's to the extremely edgy Anvil. It was more curiosity than anything else and I found it fascinating to watch the choreography of seduction, of cruising, of flirtation on every corner. 'You can't wear your key ring on your belt like that unless you're sending out a message,' said a fellow piano student whose own belt jangled with a set of keys slapping against a rather ample right buttock. (I had, in all innocence, asked someone in my early weeks in New York where I could find some fags.)

All the bars were thick with smoke – simply everyone at that time in those places smoked; but through the haze it was still possible to see. To enter Uncle Charlie's was like an audition. You would walk through the door and every eye in the place (and it was a large place) would instantly flick to the entrance to check you out, then either linger or turn away. There was nothing quite so humiliating as that one-second assessment: not even time for a smile as the handsome face's attention instantly returned to the rocks around which swished his bourbon. Some bars had TV screens which played non-stop porn. It was curious how quickly it became mere background and was barely watched by anyone. Muscles as Muzak – it was mildly ludicrous. I was in a bar once when it was raided by the police. We all moved to the back of the room and then, somehow, it was over. Twenty years earlier and I might have spent a night in prison; twenty years later and the police might have been there to *protect* the punters.

Someone I was in love with later died of AIDS. He died in shame and denial, blind from complications with the illness. I didn't know until much later. We never dated because I wasn't his type sexually, but we were close friends and used to hang out all the time and listen to records. For me to hear Keith Jarrett's *Hourglass* today is to feel physically sick with nostalgia. 'I don't know, for sex I'm just into different types of guys, I guess. Maybe it's your clothes . . .' We laughed, and kept our clothes on. Who knows, my life might have been saved by a Harris tweed jacket.

## Wisdom teeth on edge

I met Bob Neu when he was working in the ticket office at Juilliard. But as I went to so few concerts, and thus requested so few free or cheap tickets, we didn't know each other that well. Until one day in the cafeteria his pianist had let him down. 'Does anyone here play the Weber *Grand Duo Concertant*?' he asked across the table, taking a deep drag from a Merit Ultra Light cigarette. I knew it from working with a clarinettist at the RNCM so I piped up and offered to play it with him for his audition. We soon became great friends, and in the years since we've worked together in the various orchestras he has managed, from Lake Forest to Minnesota to Salt Lake City.

It has been said that *knowledge* is knowing a tomato is a fruit, and *wisdom* is knowing not to use it in a fruit salad. But what about lemons? Bob threw a party at his apartment once and I agreed to make a fruit salad. I spent much time peeling, coring, slicing, de-pipping . . . and marinating. I love the smell of lemons and I thought if I soaked them in honey they would be a nice, fresh addition to the salad. The segments were left in a honey pool overnight in Madame's fridge, then chopped up before being added to the melange. The party was going well, there was much laughter and wine and cheese and sandwiches and more wine, and then, in a large glass dish, out came the *pièce de résistance*. My fruit salad looked wholesome and delicious and the guests spooned out large, sloppy portions into bowls, perhaps adding a dollop of cream or ice cream. The jollity continued but then, all over the room, there were sudden gasps and winces as people bit into the sour lemons. Better than salt in my grandmother's sugar bowl though . . .

## The late Glenn Sales

Glenn Sales was an amazing character. He was a student of Earl Wild, a brilliant pianist, sweet, fun, absent-minded, and quite crazy at times. There was one occasion when I was due to play second piano for student auditions at CAMI Hall. I was walking calmly up the stairs of the 57th Street building when behind me appeared Glenn in a panic. He was hopelessly late to play the orchestral part for a student's Tchaikovsky First Concerto audition. We ran upstairs together and, as he threw off his coat, we could hear from inside the room the ascending dotted-rhythm D flat major chords which accompany the theme in its third appearance, after the first cadenza. He turned to me and begged me to turn pages for him and so the two of us slunk into the room, past the judges and straight over to the second piano. Glenn quickly opened the score to find the right page, plonked the music on the desk, and joined in halfway through the grand tune, to the astonishment of the auditioning pianist. He stuck around to turn my pages for two of Miss Fuschi's students and from there we went over to Saloon on Broadway for a glass of wine, meeting up by chance with Paul Verona and Angela Cheng. All was filled with laughter and such was an average day in those student days.

## Competing before Naumburg

Between the 1960s and early 1980s the winner of a major piano competition like Leeds or Cliburn or Chopin or Tchaikovsky was guaranteed a major career, or at least the brightest spotlight giving that person every chance to succeed. Those prize-winners would automatically get a manager and a record contract, both of which were tickets to fame and success in those years when recordings were impossible to clone and management relied on professional contacts . . . before the internet made promotion and recording so much more fluid and flexible. The idea that I might enter this world aged nineteen or twenty seemed impossible. And, apart from inheriting Gordon Green's suspicion about competitions, I just didn't feel ready to embark on a career. I had a few concertos and a couple of recital programmes in my fingers, but a full-time professional life seemed far off in the future.

I'd entered the internal Juilliard scholarship competition (Gina Bachauer) soon after the first semester began. I recently found a telegram sent by my father: *BEST WISHES FOR WEDNESDAY ENJOY IT THE MUSIC IS MORE IMPORTANT THAN THE PRIZE* – fourteen wise words. When, a week or so later, I discovered that I had not been selected as a winner he wrote me a remarkably touching letter, including the following observations:

> Now then. As I thought over things, it also occurred to me that this could well be a blessing. i.e. You now have no reputation to uphold continually. No selection to justify. No target to achieve regardless. Why don't you just soak up the atmosphere, take what is offered, and for goodness sake enjoy the experience. Have fun and stay away (aloof) from the trampling all around you. In time you will be able to impose your personality on your surroundings. Don't rush it. Let things come to you until you feel your feet & become known & get to know people.

I am not a parent, but as a teacher I hope I can impart such wisdom to my students.

I did enter two external competitions in 1982, in the Juilliard years: the Terence Judd Award (which I won) and Santander (where I failed to pass to the finals). The requirement for the former was an hour-long recital of free-choice repertoire held at the Wigmore Hall. I don't remember much about it except that I played 'The Gardens of Buitenzorg' from Godowsky's *Java Suite* and I was delighted when I discovered that Jorge Bolet was going to be a member of the jury. Bolet was virtually the only pianist who played Godowksy's music regularly at that time and he had known the composer, studying with his son-in-law David Saperton at the Curtis Institute. Ironically, he didn't like my playing of this three-and-a-half-minute piece and it ended up being a strike against me when the jury were deliberating. 'You were trespassing on his patch,' said one of the other jury members to me later.

The Paloma O'Shea Santander International Piano Competition was a much bigger affair with a large jury and many competitors. It was my first time at a beach outside the UK: no Walls ice cream van or saucy postcards here. I still remember the feeling of radiance from sea and sky as I stepped out of the Hotel Santemar where we were being housed. Juilliard was good preparation for this hothouse gathering of dozens of piano athletes in one place, although I still had that sense that everyone was fantastic and professional and dazzling and success-bound whereas I could barely find middle C. Many wonderful colleagues were there who became friends later – Peter Vinograde, David Korevaar, Sylvia Wang and Jean-Efflam Bavouzet. I still remember Sylvia's amazing, seductive performance of Albéniz's 'El Albaicín'. One of the other competitors asked her, quite seriously, to marry him after hearing it. And this competition was the one chance in my life to meet Mompou, who was attending. It didn't happen.

And then my name wasn't mentioned as someone in the list of finalists, so that was that. But just over a year later, on 7 December 1983, the winner, Marc Raubenheimer, died in a plane collision at Madrid airport on his way to play the final concert resulting from the prize. Countless coincidences occur every day of our lives but when I heard this tragic news I did feel a chill, and a relief that I'd not done better in Santander.

## After Naumburg

I've written before about the Naumburg competition: my terrible audition tape, the haphazard way I prepared and then played in the early rounds. My careless (actually carefree) attitude was my ticket to success. I had no nerves, just youthful excitement – and a bad cold. No room for the distraction of self-doubt. Each round passed and then I found myself in the wings of the most famous stage in the world: Carnegie Hall. It was surreal. It was 27 September 1983, I was twenty-one, starting my doctorate at Juilliard, not a care in the world, planning for many more years of gossip seated on the fourth floor's yellow carpets, when everything changed overnight. After the results were announced on stage a small group of jurors and sponsors retired to one of the rooms to the left of Stern Auditorium for a drink. (It's where I met Baroness Shirley Williams for the first time.) Adele Marcus was not there, unlike other teachers or friends. 'There's no point in entering Naumburg, dear. You're simply not ready. We have a lot more work to do.' I found a pay-phone backstage and called her. 'Miss Marcus, I just wanted to let you know that I won first prize.' A silence at the other end. Then a subdued, ever so slightly annoyed reply: 'Oh . . . well that's great, dear. Congratulations. Now, come along for your lesson as usual and we'll get to work. Goodbye.'

The following morning I was on Robert Sherman's WQXR show, *The Listening Room*, my first time playing in public in America and my first professional interview. It was an hour-long programme and involved my playing as well. Afterwards Adele phoned. 'Dear, that was *not* very impressive. Those were not the right pieces to play on the radio. When is your lesson? Oh yes, tomorrow. We have a lot to discuss.' I flinched with claustrophobia at the thought of another year of studies with her – the resentful putdowns, the irrational advice, the constant contradictions.

I went for that post-competition lesson at her apartment – she had pretty much given up going into the Juilliard building by that point. She was obviously still irritated by my success, even though she had won the same competition herself in 1928. There was no champagne from her, not even a slice of chocolate turtle pie. I had a recital debut at Alice Tully Hall in the diary, along with many other engagements: Chicago Symphony, Philadelphia Orchestra, a recording. It was a plunge in the deep end and I needed to give the organisers repertoire choices, I needed to get a Social Security card, I needed to get a manager. She couldn't help with the last two but boy could she get involved in the repertoire decisions. Over the next weeks she threw any number of programmes at me, none of them suitable, all with a constant undermining of my confidence. I just had to get away from her. I'd begun my doctorate that very month, but although I continued with the course for the rest of the academic year I was away so much playing concerts that I saw her less and less frequently.

Robert Mann, the founding first violinist of the Juilliard String Quartet, was the president of Naumburg and he had said to the jury, 'If this guy doesn't win I'm resigning from the competition.' He phoned me in the following days. 'Stephen, I want to play and record all the Beethoven sonatas with you. How about it?' I was thrilled. We began rehearsing and I began learning, both the pieces themselves, and from his wisdom in our sessions. He had as strong a personality as Adele but its creative energy was powered by a deep intelligence which fired the music.

The months beyond the competition were tough and I ended up in Lenox Hill Hospital again. I also paid a visit to Dr Leonard Moss, a psychiatrist and the husband of a concert presenter with whose orchestra I had recently played. My datebooks at the time are full of trans-Atlantic trips, sometimes more than once a fortnight, with long lists of new repertoire to be learned, and a new life to be lived away from my friends and from the security of the Juilliard hallways and practice rooms. I had a few blinding panic attacks: the first felt like my whole being was a scream and I staggered out of my apartment as if trying to escape from my very self. Added to all of this my sexuality – physical desire, but more a longing for a relationship of mutual self-giving – seemed to have no possible resolution as a Catholic. Permanently seal the tap or drown – your choice. And it was 1984, in New York. My Room 101 was AIDS. I'd only had a few sexual experiences but I was sure I was infected, sure that my life would soon be over.

Enough! It was just beginning.

# EPILOGUE

So many of the people in this book are no longer alive, especially the ones to whom I literally owe everything – my parents, my grandparents, all my piano teachers, so many precious friends. *Enough*, as well as rhyming with my often-mispronounced surname, is a line in the sand: I finish sharing my memories at the point when I start my professional career.

But writing these words of thanks forty years later, I'm aware that, in a sense, every person who has crossed my path over the years needs an acknowledgement. We are who we've met. The words with which we express ourselves (first infant gurgle to latest Google search) are not ours. We learn them. We borrow them. And writing a book is just another way of handing them on to others.

Final, specific and grateful thanks are due to a few special people: Belinda Matthews, David Godwin, Robert Davies . . . and Dennis Chang: partners in publication, and in life.